IN GOOD FAITH

IN GOOD FAITH

SECULAR PARENTING IN A RELIGIOUS WORLD

Maria Polonchek

ROWMAN & LITTLEFIELD
Lanham • Boulder • New York • London

Published by Rowman & Littlefield
A wholly owned subsidiary of The Rowman & Littlefield Publishing Group, Inc.
4501 Forbes Boulevard, Suite 200, Lanham, Maryland 20706
www.rowman.com

Unit A, Whitacre Mews, 26-34 Stannary Street, London SE11 4AB

British Library Cataloguing in Publication Information Available

Library of Congress Cataloging-in-Publication Data Available

ISBN 9781442270664 (cloth : alk. paper)
ISBN 9781442270671 (electronic)

∞™ The paper used in this publication meets the minimum requirements
of American National Standard for Information Sciences—Permanence of
Paper for Printed Library Materials, ANSI/NISO Z39.48-1992.

Printed in the United States of America

For Chris

good faith
noun

honesty or sincerity of intention

CONTENTS

CONTENTS

ACKNOWLEDGMENTS

In many ways, this book is a love letter to my various families. They started out big and have grown even bigger: to the Rolfses, Rogerses, Lupos, Coops, Poloncheks, and Weavers, thanks for folding me in.

I also want to thank my writing teachers. In the early days, Nedra Rogers and Ken Hansard lit a fire in me and the English Department at the University of Kansas gave it oxygen: Brian Daldorph, Michael Johnson, Tom Lorenz, Doug Atkins, Maryemma Graham, Giselle Anatol, and Laura Moriarty, thank you for your time and encouragement. Mahlon Coop: you sealed the deal.

Several people helped shape this book through the early drafting stage: thanks to KC MacQueen, Kelly Barth, Katie Gray, Chris Baty, and Paige Deruyscher for your graciousness and time.

Michelle Hines, Rachel Knauss, Christina McIver, Donna Hill, Brian Rusch, Amy Polonchek, Beverly Rolfs, and Crystal Belle: thanks for the loud cheering from the sidelines.

I met some incredible, inspiring people through the writing of this book. I want to thank them for giving me a glimpse into how they are making the world a better place: Dacher Keltner, Chris White, Michael Steger, Donna Schuurman, Neil Carter, Rebecca Fraser-Thill, and Dale McGowan, thank you for your contributions.

Thank you to my agent, Jennifer Unter, who has taught me so much about patience, confidence, and persistence. Thanks to Suzanne Staszak-Silva and the team at Rowman & Littlefield for taking a chance. Thank you to my publicist, Sharon Bially, for that first Skype conversation and everything that followed.

An indebted thanks to the hermits at Sky Farm, Sister Michaela and Brother Francis, for sharing the wild turkeys, single bed, and blazing Sonoma sunshine.

Katie Savage: I can't even. Thank you for your help with this book, but especially for just seeing me—always—and going with it.

Finally, the acknowledgments that won't do justice for what has been given. To my mom: the specifics are impossible to list. To Chris, for being an incredible human being, one I'm so lucky to have met. You believe in me when I so often don't believe in myself. Big league. And to Luke, Taj, and Sola: the three of you may never know just how much you've given me. You've encouraged me to grow in so many ways. You've been so generous with your time and love and minds, without even realizing it. You inspire me to do better. Thank you.

INTRODUCTION

On Making It Personal

Illumination can emerge from asking the right questions, even if answers are not to be found.

—Michael Krasny

It's unprecedented, the number of people in this country who will publicly admit that they're not religious. It's unprecedented, too, the amount of information we have at our fingertips instructing us on how to raise children. This is why I was surprised one Easter Sunday, after a distressing morning visiting church with extended family, when a quick Google search didn't bring me much on raising children without religion. Google usually brings me everything.

This particular weekend we were away from our home in the San Francisco Bay Area, visiting my brothers, sisters, nieces, and nephews, and we went with them to church. My siblings, our spouses, our kids: we're close. We're lucky. Originally Midwesterners, most of us are now scattered up and down the California coast and make it a point to gather at least a few times a year. I've heard the stories of families who don't get along and people who dread holidays and reunions. This has not been my experience, and I'm incredibly grateful. It's not that we've sailed through family life on calm water; we've experienced our share of pain and grief. And like the tide to the shore, our connections to one another ebb and flow. But love, joy, and hope create room for temporal grace, and it's in this space that we meet.

When my husband, Chris, and I visit family, we want to experience their lives. We sleep in their homes, visit the places they work and go to school, eat in their favorite restaurants. On Easter, we wanted to attend their church: my brother, a musician, plays in the band, and we know that church is an important part of who they are. After all, they spend more time with members of the congregation than they do with us.

My siblings and I grew up as children in an evangelical Christian home, and all of us have further constructed our own beliefs as adults, some of us staying closer to the original trail than others. I may be the furthest away, an apostate now and secular humanist, definitely a *nonbeliever*, though I rarely offer my private thoughts about religion in a group setting, even (especially?) with family. As someone who doesn't believe in God at all, I find little to contribute to my siblings' nuanced debates over their respective Christian beliefs. Most of the time, these debates are kept to a minimum, and the brief detachment I experience as a nonbeliever is short-lived.

Up until this Easter service, the only other church services my children had attended were during Christmas at the Episcopal church of my husband's childhood. They had fun placing stuffed animals next to a manger at the altar and eating through tiny raisin boxes during the service. Back at their grandparents' house, they played with little figurines in the decorative nativity scene and cooed over baby Jesus.

For Easter Sunday at my brother's, the kids asked to go to the children's church service with their cousins, who promised magic markers and cookies in abundance. Chris and I agreed beforehand that attending church would be a learning experience for them and, being familiar with the message of most evangelical churches, I confirmed with my sister-in-law that the sermons at this particular one were generally positive and gentle. What harm would children's church do? I dropped the kids off in their assigned room, settled into the adult service with the deep breath I can take during a break from three young children, and beamed with pride as my brother played his guitar in the band. *This isn't so bad,* I thought, feeling only slightly alarmed when the sermon focused on the inherent deficiency of mankind.

Oh, how it hit me after the service, then, when I collected the kids and my daughter, who was four at the time, who had rarely even seen commercials on television because I'd been so protective of what she heard, asked,

"Did you know that baby Jesus grew up into a poor, hairy man who was kidnapped and beaten with leather straps?"

What she said after that has become a blur in my memory, but it involved a spiky crown, nails, and blood. Lots of blood.

Dear reader, depending on your own experience, your reaction to the events of that morning may be different from my own.

"I can't believe this!"

"What did you expect?"

"At least someone out there told your children the Truth."

And in fact, my reaction was a bit of all three: *I can't believe this! What did I expect?* And even *Someone out there just thinks they are telling my children the Truth.*

Several hours later, after addressing this new information with the help of my cool-headed husband, cooking up an Easter dinner, and tossing some plastic eggs in the yard for a hunt, I sneaked away with Google, feeling panicked, confused, and, yes, angry. I typed *raising kids without religion.*

I found several online sources—blogs, forums, websites—but I was looking for books. A good, long book. Something I could hold in my hands. For as long as I can remember, books have been a place to go, provided people to be with, offered ideas to share when I'm feeling most alone in the world. Two came up repeatedly and exclusively: Dale McGowan's groundbreaking *Parenting beyond Belief* and the follow-up guide *Raising Freethinkers.* When we returned home that week, I immediately checked out both from the library and found that, while they were helpful and encouraging, they only whetted my appetite for more. McGowan's books are anthologies, collections of writings from various authors, and I was looking for something that could take me on a longer, more personal journey.

Because it is personal, isn't it? Having children takes us back to our own childhoods, opens doors we thought were closed: memories, fears, dreams, desires, beliefs. No matter how sophisticated and rational our ideas seem to us now, our children remind us that our lived experiences—those events from our pasts that shape our perspectives—also influence those ideas.

I come from an intense, transformative, identity-shaping religious background. That's my experience. Now, I live an intense, transformative, identity-shaping secular life. That's my experience, too. Having traveled between two extremes, and along most of the spectrum that falls in between, I find myself now with a peculiar worldview. I can *almost* always empathize with both sides of a debate. I'm able to slip into a traditional, conservative church service in the Bible Belt and connect with the people there almost as easily as I'll join a radical, progressive protest rally on the West Coast and connect with people there.

Notice, though: it's the *people* I want to connect with. Not their religions, agendas, or rules. What makes us a gift to one another is what we bring through experience, thoughtfulness, and curiosity. Unfortunately, our culture doesn't value nuance as much as extremes, and so I often feel a little . . . left out. Ironically, it's having kids and joining the ranks of parenthood that has me asking now, more than ever, *Where are more people like me?*

Where I live, in northern California, it's not hard to find people who feel like they don't fit in. I started asking around and found that many parents with whom I cross paths are grappling with the religion issue, but we're grappling in different ways. Most of us are, if not from a different part of the world, from different parts of this country. We've gotten here in different ways, from different places, but here we are: starting families and raising our children without the religious foundations and institutions with which we, ourselves, were raised. At best, this predicament can cause some confusion, distance, or guilt; at worst, we run into grief, alienation, and rage.

If you are a thinking person, you are learning, growing, changing. Always. For a very long time, those changes are your own. You make your own decisions; you are the primary beneficiary of your own ideas. You get used to this autonomy, and then, suddenly, you have another human being in your care and your life isn't exactly your own anymore. Many of us will admit that we had no idea what this parenting gig would be like until we were in it. Many of us, as curious and critical as we are, have taken a few things for granted about growing up with some type of religious framework. And most of us have lived for some time without having someone who trusts Every. Single. Thing. we say stop us during dinner to ask what happens when we die. We used to be able to drive to the store without having to explain how the universe was formed. We used to take showers and brush our teeth and sit on the toilet without having someone run in the room asking, "Is God everywhere?"

The book you hold now is inspired by my own search for answers as a nonreligious parent from a religious background in a religious world. In the writing of this book, I've quickly discovered that my search for "parenting without religion" isn't really what I am searching for. There is no way to simply *avoid* religion as a parent, perhaps the first of my many mistaken assumptions. A more accurate description of what I'm looking for is "parenting without *a* religion," or, to better express the way it feels not to belong in the status quo, "parenting *outside* of religion."

This book travels one more leg in the exhilarating, frightening, fulfilling journey of being entrusted with our world's children.

SOME THOUGHTS ON LANGUAGE

The most common question people ask when I describe a book about parenting outside of religion is "What about parents who are spiritual but not religious?"

If we were all working with the same understanding of what that means, it would be much easier to answer this question. The short answer is, yes, this book is for you. My hope is *anyone* with a curious mind, wherever they fall on the spectrum of religiosity, will find something of value in the following pages.

However, it's pretty impossible to write about the topics of spirituality, religion, and belief without running into the confusions and limitations of language. As a writer, I find words simultaneously invaluable and infuriating. I'm preoccupied with getting them right; one might say I'm obsessed. Just to construct the second sentence of this paragraph, I looked up the definition of *words*, *invaluable*, and *infuriating* to make sure I'm writing what I'm thinking. I accept that I won't always articulate my thoughts well in speech, but, perhaps, there's a chance I can do it when I write.

As if my relationship with words weren't complicated enough, I've decided to write about subjects that are, at best, commonly misunderstood and, at their most challenging, ineffable (which is a word that I learned in my search for a word that means "too great or extreme to be expressed or described in words").

At first, I didn't realize I was up against ineffability. I knew my subjects—parenting and religion—were complicated, in the primary definition:

difficult to analyze, understand, or explain. But the secondary definition most captures the nature of their complication: *consisting of parts intricately combined.* These intricately combined parts are the ones that are ineffable; otherwise I'd list them for you.

Because of the complicated nature of these subjects, what I intend when using a word may be very different from what the reader hears. I'm particularly sensitive to this fact after growing up *not* knowing the correct definitions and descriptions of certain words. I can't simply void the parts of my memory that consider some of the words I've used to describe myself as an adult—secular, atheist, humanist—as Very Bad Things. It's because of my previous ignorance that I attempt to embrace the labels now, as I hope my existence might correct even one person's misunderstanding of what these words mean.

But back to *spiritual.* The definition of *spirit* is "the nonphysical part of a person that is the seat of emotions and character," so, technically, any living person is "spiritual."[1] However, it's common for people to describe themselves as "spiritual but not religious," which implies some people are *not* spiritual. This conflation between religion and spirituality causes the word to mean something almost entirely different to everyone, which is why I either avoid it or make sure I understand how another person is using it.

What it comes down to, for the purposes of this book, is that *all* of us are capable of nurturing the parts of our minds concerned with difficult questions outside the immediate moment, and, in that way, all of us are spiritual with the potential for further development. We don't *have* to embrace this part of ourselves, to indulge in these questions, to identify in this way, but our children often do, from the time they can string words together in a sentence.

Labels are handy in that they give us a way to identity and fit into something; they are also damning in that they give *others* a way to identify *us,* and few of us fit into labels neatly. We know what parts of ourselves spill outside the lines, but others may not.

This world of definitions is not a positive one for nonbelievers: there's that prefix again, *non-.* Because religious or supernatural belief is the default position of the majority in our culture, those of us who are just "nones" (which is what the Pew Research Center calls people with no religious affiliation) must continue to define ourselves by what we are not, the implication being that we are lacking.[2] *Not* religious. *Without* God. *Non/Un/Dis*-believers. But my preference to reject magic or superstition is hardly what defines me, which is why I continue to search for and try on words to describe what I *am* rather than what I'm *not*—why, even though *atheist, nonbeliever*, or *none* all describe my relationship to the supernatural, I would rather use them only in the instances when nothing else will do.

A word I didn't consider very relevant until the writing of this book—another one I used to think was Very Bad—is *apostate*. An apostate is "a person who renounces a religious or political belief or principle."[3] This label gives us loads of helpful information at once: not only does the person *not* subscribe to a religion, but we also know that she once *did*. I find describing and thinking of myself in this way incredibly helpful; because my identity as a child was so rooted in the religion given to me, my identity as an adult is rooted in my deconversion. Understanding that a person once belonged in a different category lets us know that her experiences have another layer to them. In this case, it's a more personal, emotional layer than is experienced by those who have not gone through such a change.

Why do these definitions matter so much, and what do they have to do with raising kids? In the first and second chapters, I will discuss how coming to terms with our relationships to religion and how we define ourselves currently very much impacts the journey for our children; in the next section, chapters 3–6, I'll look at those existential topics historically monopolized and defined by religion and consider and learn about them in secular, nonreligious ways; finally, in the last two chapters, I return to the personal, exploring identity through the way our roots and traditions continue to define us. For now, know this: no matter which of the definitions here resonates most with you, no matter where you fall along the spectrum, there is a place for you here, and, together, we will create a place for our children.

1

BAGGAGE CLAIM

I am still every age that I have been.

—Madeleine L'Engle

In the sea of advice I sought and received when I was pregnant for the first time ten years ago, I clung to one like a life preserver and still repeat to this day: "It doesn't all happen at once." Raising a child will include sleepless nights, teething pain, potty training, giggles, tantrums, first times, last times, suffering, joy, fulfillment, anguish, holding on, letting go—but it doesn't all happen simultaneously. I don't remember who said this to me, or when, exactly, but I'm guessing I'd asked the person about diaper rash and driving permits in the same breath, with a big belly and wild eyes.

It's common sense, this advice; it seems so simple and obvious . . . now. But before I was in the thick of them, those sleepless nights, before I learned to take each contraction, and then each stage, as it comes, I had this time of anticipation when I could do nothing about the imminent change except read books and ask questions. At the time, I was working as the equipment buyer for an outdoor adventure retailer. I spent my days contemplating specs, considering reviews, testing samples. The customer wanted to know about worst-case scenarios: which tent sets up fastest in the rain; which roller bag can handle cobblestone streets; which kayak is easiest to roll. I knew babies weren't exactly like a tent or a kayak, but I prepared for having them in the same way.

Once I received that advice—*It doesn't all happen at once*—I immediately embraced the one-step-at-a-time mind-set and returned the books on the first year of school and making it through adolescence. Around the same time, we learned we were having twins, and the emphasis on simple survival became even more practical and pertinent. I focused my attention on birthing, feeding, and sleeping: existential questions could wait. My husband, Chris, and I hadn't discussed, or even really thought much about, religion since our early days of dating, when we happily realized we had more in common than not regarding our lack of belief in the supernatural. Our day-to-day focus was on the essentials, and the tackling of it, based on research and preparation. Is this why I was caught off guard and tripped over my own thoughts when the twins were around three years old and one of them asked over a spaghetti dinner, "Who is God?"

Since that evening, I've discovered there are questions my kids ask that I can easily answer. "What is your favorite dinosaur?" for example, or "Where does the sun go at night?" These are the questions I hear in my ears, and they stay in the general vicinity of my brain. They don't evoke an emotional response; they don't stir up memories from my past. If I don't know the answer, I can say, "Why don't we find out together?" and reach for Google.

And then there are certain questions my kids ask that paralyze me. I certainly wish it weren't so, but when I hear them, the words shoot straight from my head, past my heart, into my gut. I find myself feeling angry, or sad, or confused. I recall experiences, emotions, ideas that I haven't confronted in a very long time. And, well, good luck looking any of them up.

"Who is God?" is one of these questions.

But my children? They don't understand this difference. How is "Who is God?" so different from "What is your favorite dinosaur?" Why do certain questions make me stammer and fidget and give long answers that no one can understand?

I can only envy Chris's calm, thoughtful, articulate responses to our children's questions. His disposition is naturally less reactive and more even-tempered than mine, but he also has a different lived experience. Our experiences inform our worldview and the way we respond to others, especially our children. In their book *Parenting from the Inside Out*, authors Daniel Siegel and Mary Hartzell use neurobiology and attachment research to explore an idea many of us have suspected: our own childhoods have an enormous effect on the way we parent. The authors write, "By making sense of our lives we can deepen a capacity for self-understanding and bring coherence to our emotional experience, our views of the world, and our interactions with our children."[1]

Indeed, it took my husband pointing out how peculiar my reactions are to certain questions for me to realize that I needed to address some personal issues. If we want to be our children's primary educators (because there will be many more) on such culturally tangled topics as religion, philosophy, spirituality, morality, and sexuality, we must confront our own sticky histories. Children ask questions. As critical thinkers ourselves, we *want* them to ask questions. Dale McGowan, a trailblazer for nonreligious families, recalls in *Parenting beyond Belief* that his daughter once asked seventy-eight questions in two hours.[2] I'd never thought to count, myself, but I've learned that the questions can go from "Where do butterflies sleep?" to "What happens when we die?" very quickly.

When I realized we were getting up to McGowan's 39 QPH (questions per hour), I *tried* looking up the right ways to answer their philosophical questions. But for as much information on parenting styles and techniques that's available, the proverbial shelf that houses "How to Answer Existential Questions in Ways Your Child Will Understand" is scant. Even when I have found information that should be helpful to me, theoretically speaking—for parents who are raising their children outside of religion—it hasn't always resonated, for reasons that are just becoming clear.

What I was taught about religion as a child and the religion in which I was raised contributes to my sense of self, the very self I'm working to understand for my children's sake and my own. I was raised in an evangelical Christian household and, though I may no longer identify this way, I find it impossible to consider Christianity, religion, and spirituality in general without enfolding my deep connection to it. My experience explains why I so strongly believe that no child should be indoctrinated with one religious truth and why parents, religious or not, must explore ways to address religious influence all around us.

Call me now what you will: a non/un/dis-believer, a heretic, a heathen, a doubter, a skeptic, a freethinker, an apostate. You can call me an atheist, though even atheists can't agree on how to define the word, so I'm not sure we will. Whatever you decide to call me, understand that, as a child, I was taught and *very much believed* that whatever I am now—which is decidedly *not* Christian—was the worst kind of person one could be. And this little girl, who was brought up in an evangelical Christian home, is still nested inside my being, whispering, *Don't forget about me.*

I hear the voices, too, of friends and family who have influenced me and shared in my experiences along the way, many of whom have stayed on a path I've left but remain a part of my life, part of my children's lives. So when I look to sources with whom I identity *now* on religious matters—other secular, agnostic, or atheist thinkers—my current, rational brain agrees, but I'm stifling a voice from inside, a self saying to myself, *But I was taught what's real and true!*

Our childhoods are recalled through a foggy lens, but they are still our experience, part of our very being. Somewhere along the way to becoming adult, many of us learn to trivialize the childhood experience, to call it "cute" and "sweet" and dismiss it as nothing serious. But having children reminds me of the child I was: the ardor with which I took my minutes and hours. I was goofy, too, of course, just like I am sometimes today, but I remember how deeply I felt, how many questions I asked, how badly I wanted to understand. When my children laugh or sob with all of their bodies, I'm reminded how uncaring and cruel it feels to a child to be dismissed as "silly" or "dramatic."

I will not, cannot, easily dismiss the child I was by the adult I've become. In order to glean insight from the freethinkers, atheists, agnostics, humanists, and nonbelievers I look to now, and raise my children as thoughtfully and responsibly as I can, I must reconcile the experience of my childhood and my experiences since those days.

I have baggage from my past, and I need to claim it.

I grew up in a Christian home and attended Christian churches that were so fundamental in nature even they wouldn't agree to be associated with one another. We moved often—every year or two—which is why there were so many new churches, usually the most conservative in a tricounty area. One thing all of these churches had in common was that they were evangelical, in the frequently understood four-part definition of the word: they believed in (1) the ultimate authority of the Bible as the word of God, (2) the atonement of Christ's crucifixion, (3) the need for personal salvation, and (4) the mission to convert others.

The churches I grew up in were unwavering in their assertions of the Truth and unyielding in their denial that any other church could provide the road to salvation. This explains why I felt my first flood of confusion, then fear, then despair over my religion when I was around eight years old, after driving by a Catholic cemetery. We'd just moved back to Kansas from Texas and were on our way to a family reunion. (I spent much of my time at this reunion studying the backside of a woman recently married into the family who, I'd heard my aunt whisper to my mother, was not wearing any underwear. How could she *tell*?)

After passing the tombstones spread out on an open western Kansas plain, I asked the grown-ups in the car a question:

"Why did that cross have Jesus on it?"

I had never seen a crucifix before. The empty cross I knew so well, the one that stood for joy and hope and made me feel safe and welcomed whenever I saw it, had a bloodied, punctured, limp Jesus on it. Jesus, who, yes, was crucified, but who came back to life after three days and joined his Father in heaven. Seeing this Jesus stuck to his cross in the middle of a bunch of tombstones wasn't just confusing. It was terrifying. Surely this was the site of the occult, I thought.

A child of the 1980s, I learned about the occult through schoolyard rumors during our two years in southern Texas and considered myself something of an expert. They were made up of people who wore black makeup and clothes and worshipped Satan; they wanted to kill little blonde girls for fun (thank God I was brunette!) and lured them with candy and used them for human sacrifice. Was this a burial ground?

"That's a Catholic cemetery. Catholicism is another religion."

"They're not Christian?" I asked.

"No."

The answer I was given may surprise readers not familiar with fundamental Protestant denominations (as opposed to Mainline Protestants), as it surprised me, years later, when I learned the Catholic Church was, in fact, the first widespread Christian church. This particular lesson about Catholicism and the confusion that followed may have been the first loose thread in my eventual religious unraveling. It stands out in my mind, even though I don't remember which grown-up answered my question. The grown-ups from my childhood blur together into a hazy, floating mass of information, hovering on the periphery of the sphere that was my world. Whether it was my mother, my father, an aunt or an uncle, or someone from church, I understand now that they answered my questions using what they believed to be true. But after the information leaves the mouth of one person and enters the mind of another . . . well, we all have our own interpretations. Even the way I remember it now has been twisted and turned over by time and experience.

"And only Catholics can be buried in their cemeteries?"

"Yes."

"Why do they have a cross with Jesus on it?"

"They don't celebrate his resurrection. They focus on his death. It's very negative."

"How do you know so much about Catholics?"

"My best friend was Catholic when I was a kid."

"Do Catholics go to heaven?"

"We don't know. We really don't know. . . . We'll just have to pray for them."

The implications I considered after this conversation were seeds planted deep in my consciousness—in my gut or my head or my heart—somewhere within, where the swirls of consciousness exist. I didn't doubt what I was told, but I felt—sensed before I knew—that something wasn't right, or, if it was, it was terribly wrong. I believed what the grown-ups told me, but as a child what I believed wasn't really *belief*—confidence in the existence of something not susceptible to proof—so much as it's just The Way It Is. Because of my age and disposition, instead of doubting or questioning, I worried. If I were to choose one noun that defines my childhood religious experience, it is this: *worry*.

All those people, buried there, and they might not be in heaven? But didn't they think they were going to heaven, just like I did? What about their family members, the ones who might not be Catholic?

"What if someone wants to be buried there who isn't Catholic?"

"Why would someone want to do that?"

"Well, if they are family."

My mouth went dry, my stomach knotted, at the thought that families might not end up together in the afterlife. Because we moved often, friends and neighbors came and went, but my family—not just my parents and brothers and sister (there were five of us kids) but also my maternal grandparents, aunts, uncles, too many cousins to count—even though I saw some only a few times a year, they were my world. No matter how many times we moved, they were always still there.

Just a handful of extended family members were not part of the evangelical conversion that took place on my mother's side of the family before I was born, so through the years and hushed whispers I learned of some who may have strayed or never accepted Jesus in the first place. The idea that an aunt or a liberal-college-attending brother might not be in heaven with me kept me awake at night, sometimes crying through my prayers. My prayers as a child were not gentle thank-yous and requests. They were begging, pleading, bargaining.

One family member in particular, my mom's oldest sister, was a source of great mystery and worry for me. Of the people in the descending ranks of Less Likely to Go to Heaven—Methodists, Lutherans, Catholics, Jehovah's Witnesses, Mormons (remember, I hadn't yet learned there were religions outside American Christianity)—atheists were at the bottom. In my understanding, people who had the nerve not to believe in God were synonymous with the Texas occult members—and clearly going to hell. Yet the two things I knew about my aunt from family whisperings was that she was a bona fide genius (*her IQ test couldn't be scored because she didn't miss anything!*) and that she was an atheist. I studied her from a safe distance, watched her talk and laugh. She seemed so normal. And nice. She looked like the rest of us—fair Irish complexion, dark French hair, strong German bones—with a sweet smile, kind eyes, and gentle manner. How could she not believe in God? But I couldn't ask: this much was clear. The only stories we told and questions we asked about religion needed to conclude with a testimony of salvation.

As a child, I could describe my family as a lot of things—big, loud, late, strange, fun—but, above all, they were kind. My grandfather taught my mother, who taught me, in no uncertain terms, that the color of a person's skin does not make a difference in how they should be treated. Nor do the clothes they wear or car they drive. (Which was good, because we all had cheap clothes and shitty cars.) That the most important thing in your day is how you make others feel. That we bear one another's burdens.

This legacy of kindness extended not only to people who look or live differently from us but also to those who believed differently as well. Kindness, which begets acceptance, was the line that seems to separate my family from angry, combative, argumentative evangelical Christians I've encountered in the years since. Certainly I was taught to be a witness for Christ to others, to spread the Good News, but, above all, kindness was the reason that we invited anyone from exchange students to the homeless to our holiday gatherings.

Religious tradition permeated our holidays, but these were also times my worldview expanded. My family doesn't limit our tight bond to the biologic: anyone who didn't have a place to go when work or campus shut down for the day was welcomed at our proverbial table. Thanksgiving and Christmas was a time for us kids to meet someone who might not have a family or a house, or who had these things but across the world.

Is this kindness what brought my aunt, the Atheist, home, year after year, to comply with long-winded prayers, living-room Bible studies, stories of visions, messages, miracles? Does unwavering kindness explain how she patiently listened to her daughter's stories of time spent with cousins going to Vacation Bible School, accepting Jesus, getting baptized? Is the accumulation of kindness what gave her the dignity, through burning cheeks, to remain one of the only people seated at my grandfather's funeral after the preacher instructed those of us who were saved and would join him in heaven to please stand?

I think so. I think it may be. Kindness, yes, and love.

And even though *worry* is the first noun I would choose to define my childhood religious experience, *acceptance* would be the second. Given my family's ways—big, loud, late, strange, fun—it's no wonder they can often be found on the fringes, that a nice, quiet, calm religion is not where people go when the awe and pain and wonder and fear and gratitude of life sends them searching for a place where they don't feel alone.

There's no way around this: my family was poor. At times, the cars we drove left pieces behind on the street; at times, I stole toilet paper from public restrooms to bring home; at times, I hid illness from my parents because I knew we couldn't afford to see a doctor. Things my children take for granted were special luxuries to me as a child—batteries, stamps, tape. Being one of the kids who got free lunch cards kept me from feeling like I belonged at school, but I was sure I belonged at least two places: with my family and with my church. I loved using the vernacular people around me understood and celebrated: congregation, testimony, salvation, sin, miracle, temptation, fellowship, communion. And the King James Version of the Bible we were required to read? I loved the language: *whosoever*, *ye*, *wherein*, *verily*, *brethren*. Such a vocabulary for a little girl!

We went to church Sunday morning, Sunday night, and Wednesday night, and those were my favorite parts of the week. I brought my white leather Bible—a splurge from my mom when I was baptized that had my name on the cover inscribed in gold (*In Gold!*)—a notebook, and a pen. Often, on a Sunday afternoon or a Wednesday night, there would be a potluck following the service. For a girl who didn't have much money and parents who didn't spend much time in the kitchen, the potlucks were feasts. The cheesy casseroles! The juice! The desserts!

A memory that still makes me feel cherished and safe, one of my earliest, when I was six or seven: my mother surprising my sister and me with pastel Easter dresses and hats with ribbons. Nudging us awake in the dark without much effort because we were thrilled to dress in the quiet and ride along in the backseat to the sunrise service, where we stood with the grown-ups in a circle on a hilltop to sing hymns, holding hands that were so warm despite the chill in the Texas spring air, feeling exceptional because not many children get to witness a brilliant pink-orange sky with such peace and beauty. I experienced this moment in awe, and at the time I believed what I was told: awe is impossible without God.

All of that kindness and acceptance radiating from my extended family and church congregation doesn't change the fact that I was taught that whoever has not accepted Jesus as their savior would go to hell. And I worried about hell. A lot. Not that I would go, myself, because I was saved. Of this, I was sure. But I worried about others. There were lots of logistics, guidelines, I learned, regarding who would make it and who wouldn't. For a while, the talk of the family was that one of my older brothers was no longer saved after he went to college.

(My aunt, my brother . . . how did I know these things? No one ever told me outright, nor did the adults discuss difficult things with one another explicitly. But isn't this the way of a child, to pick up much more information than she's given credit for? Isn't this the way of a family, through the years and generations, to just know what they know? Like the game of telephone, where the whispers distort the content of the message: Who started it? Is this what they really said?)

I asked around about what happens if someone is a Christian and then changes his mind. I learned about the "final perseverance of the saints" (the Baptist take on a Catholic doctrine): that once a person is saved, he is always saved. My brother had accepted Jesus years ago, and this reserved his spot in heaven.

Yes, I liked this answer. It was a relief to me. Until I thought about it more. What about a murderer? What if someone had accepted Jesus when he was young, grew up and changed his mind, and then murdered someone? What if this person is in jail, right now, awaiting the death penalty? Would God still let him in, like he would my brother, who may or may not have changed his mind?

But I often didn't ask more questions after thinking things through. This became a pattern I struggled with for years to come: someone answers my questions with an abstraction, gives me a book to read full of metaphors, and instructs me to pray, have faith, and trust, but those answers only create more questions. It would take a long time for me accept that no one actually had answers—that the questions were the thing.

In the meantime, on my childhood list of people who would go to heaven:

1. those who accept Jesus as their personal savior and are baptized
2. most probably those who accept Jesus and are baptized, even if later they change their minds, unless they do something really bad, like murder someone

That meant my family would all be there, even my aunt, who I was sure would come around if I prayed for her really hard. She might be a genius, but she obviously had not thought this one through.

On my list of who wouldn't go to heaven:

1. atheists (unless they came around, like my aunt would)
2. probably Catholics
3. animals (I remember it being difficult for the adult who broke this news to me)

But there were some very big gaps on my lists: babies, people who hadn't heard the Good News and thus couldn't accept Jesus, and anyone who died in a car wreck on the way to being baptized. (Admittedly, there were very few in this last category, but, I argued, it could happen.)

My church taught that, in order to be saved, one must ask Jesus into her heart and be fully immersed in water, symbolic of the death, burial, and resurrection of Christ. (Ideally, it would be murky water, like a river or lake. But in a pinch, the YMCA swimming pool would do, which was my preference.)

The logistics of this path to salvation and heaven worked for everyone I personally knew, but even at an early age I was painfully aware that there were plenty of people out there I didn't know. For a girl who wouldn't travel outside a four-state radius until high school, my consciousness of the furthest reaches of the globe was peculiar. What about the people who died a bit too soon or were born in the wrong place? These were questions I asked over and over and was told some version of the message: Trust that God knows best.

Because the adults in my life were the conduit through which I connected to God, when I began to doubt them I began to doubt him. (Him! Of course he's a man in the clouds wearing robes and sporting a gray beard. Children are literal, concrete thinkers. When I was taught about Adam and Eve, heaven and hell, Noah and the flood, and the near-sacrifice of Isaac by Abraham, I wasn't mulling over metaphors and symbolism. I was gripped with a toxic combination of fascination and fear.)

Several years after the drive by the Catholic cemetery, I found myself living in a predominantly Catholic town. After all the moving around during my elementary school years, by the time I was thirteen we landed in a small town near the Nebraska border where I would spend the next five. Despite having a population of no more than three thousand, it supported two elementary schools: public and Catholic. The Catholic Church was in the center of town, and in junior high many of my new schoolmates were Catholic. Never one to back away from religious discussions, I was both cautious and curious, and soon enough I came to understand that what I was told as a child about Catholicism might be open for debate.

During high school, as my mother's commitment to the Assembly of God church waned and my relationships with Catholic friends bloomed, I finally attended my first mass. The richness and patina of the service was like nothing I'd ever experienced. Instead of the unconfined, loosey-goosey conduct during worship I was used to, mass required circumscribed, concordant behavior. I found it novel and comforting, this unspoken understanding among such a large congregation. I loved kneeling on risers when others kneeled, making the sign of the cross in unison. To a girl who wanted nothing more than to fit in, this type of service was just the ticket to belonging. I was eager to join the line for communion when my friend's mother gently touched my shoulder.

"You aren't supposed to take communion," she whispered.

I was crestfallen.

"Why?"

Her touch was loving, her voice warm. But she had to tell me: "You haven't been confirmed into the true church."

Her understanding of Catholicism as the true church, combined with the explanation from my childhood, that Catholics are not Christian, clearly did not add up. The adults I trusted did not agree about some fundamental issues. And if they were wrong about these issues, what else might they be wrong about?

Worry. Acceptance. Awe. Fear. Doubt. These moments—snapshots of religion and spirituality through my childhood—what am I to make of them? That growing up in a fundamentalist faith encompasses such a wide range of emotions, from the positive to the negative, is difficult for some people to understand. Many people, especially those with an agenda or, ironically, their own insecurities, want to insist on one interpretation of my experience: Wasn't it so messed up? Aren't I glad I left it all behind? And yes, I do answer with the affirmative to those questions *and* answer with the affirmative to others: Didn't I feel a sense of belonging? Wasn't I influenced by some loving teachers? I emphasize my ambivalence here because it's often dismissed or even impossible for some people to understand, which only stalls our ability to have constructive conversations about religion and, especially, its effects on a child.

So, what do I believe now, how did I arrive here, and how do I know that I have it any more correct than my teachers did? How does my experience relate to anyone who had it better or worse, or—here's a lovely thought— neutral, when it comes to religion?

Before I continue with those questions, I must confess: writing about my deconversion is difficult. It's not that I'm ashamed or unsure. It's just that these thoughts, experiences, and travails are more intimate for me than almost anything else in my life: sacred, even, though without evoking the divine. The thoughts I have been free to form as an adult are most precious to me. But I also have insider knowledge about what many people think of a nonbeliever. It pains me to think that believers in my life might refuse to see me as a complete person who doesn't need saving, or pity me as a damaged person with an unfortunate experience. These are the ways I was taught to view people like me when I was young. My human desire to be part of a group, to be accepted for who I am, makes it very difficult to discuss my doubt so openly. Combine that knowledge with the grieving process of losing religion, and one can understand why the whole subject is so fraught.

The grieving process? Actually, yes. Make no mistake: losing one's religion is a deep loss. It's painful. It hurts, in those ethereal places within that absorb shock and cause us to double over, mourning a part of ourselves. As author and agnostic Michael Krasny asks in *Spiritual Envy*, a memoir in which he devotes a significant portion recalling the entity he knew as a child, "How can I or anyone else make up for the loss of a God who once felt real, comforting, close and personal?"[3]

I've heard from and read about countless others who describe losing their religion this way. With an unprecedented number of people in our country identifying as "nonreligious," support groups such as Recovering from Religion are being established and recognizing the difficulty of this process. We are grieving and often angry at no real target because the religious identities we grieve were not cultivated by our choice in the first place.

What makes it so hard? Aside from the almost inexplicable loss of identity taken from one's core, it's also a lonely, alienating process. In all of the religious revivals, retreats, baptisms, dedications, and celebrations I've participated in, I'm one of many, cheering for and encouraging and supporting a fellow human being. In deconversion, that built-in support is gone. Vanished. There is only silence, if you're one of the lucky ones.

It's the difficulties I faced during my deconversion, the pain I've experienced getting here, and reconciling who I am now as a person I was taught to fear as a child: it's for this reason I find raising children to accept the teachings of any one religion before they have the cognitive development to question those teachings morally unsound. We will make many mistakes as parents, but forcing a religious identity upon our children doesn't have to be one of them.

It comes down, I suppose, to consent. Children are not able to give consent on these matters, and we would do well to respect this dilemma. Our culture takes the concept "consent" seriously, from sexual conduct to cultural appropriation to reproductive issues. Being empowered to offer consent on such formative experiences is what cultivates and honors human dignity. Of course, your belief system will inform your views on human dignity, but many people, religious and secular alike, will agree that every person has inherent dignity and should be given the chance to fully realize it.

Religion can confuse and hijack a child's life, in ways her teachers would never anticipate or intend. Tracking the journey of the person who most influenced my own journey—my mother's—it's clear to me now that an individual's search for truth is dynamic. It's always changing, whether those changes are massive or imperceptible. Adults often take for granted our ability to grow, evolve, adjust, and forget that, for a time, our children are watching and absorbing these particular steps in our journey to be static, concrete, inflexible.

Deconversion stories don't have the zing to them that conversion stories do. Losing one's religion can be a slow, sometimes dull, meandering process, lacking the excitement of supernatural signs, images, and voices that often work their way into testimonies of salvation. Deconversion stories include lots of time spent thinking, asking questions, reading, observing, and thinking some more. Results are often inconclusive. Not the stuff of a blockbuster movie or best-selling "how-to."

Earlier I described the drive by the cemetery as the first loose thread in my religious unraveling. If religion works like a sweater that someone else puts on you for protection from the elements, I found mine had many loose threads. I pulled at them and, sometimes, pulled hard. At times, I might begin to feel a chill and quickly attempt to mend the holes, only to have a thread unravel somewhere else. Even when I took the whole thing off, for a long time I carried it with me to put back on when I stood out or felt cold. It would take years to set down the bulk entirely.

The heaven/hell confusion during my high school years constituted an entire hemline on my sweater and made the rest pretty easy to undo. After I realized that even other Christians couldn't agree on who was saved and that human error might be responsible for much of mankind spending an afterlife in hell, my covering became very thin. Where we spend the afterlife—and whether there *is*, in fact, an afterlife—had, perhaps, the largest influence on what I believed as a child. By high school, I'd decided that if my atheist aunt, or a baby born in China, or my Catholic best friend were going to hell, then I would not fear hell. I would just as well go, too.

Letting go of this fear of hell and preoccupation with an afterlife quickly changed my understanding of God. If he was, in fact, a god who had such a vague and complicated plan, whether he's the God of the Old Testament, who would be so judgmental and ruthless, or the God of the New Testament, who had screwed up so badly that someone needed be tortured and murdered to make up for it, he was no god for me. But that didn't mean I was ready to stop believing altogether; I just wanted to know what other ideas of God looked like. By the time I got to college, I was ready to consider other options when, my first week there, a campus ministry leader called me up on my dorm room telephone and invited me to his group. Someone from my hometown, no doubt someone who was worried about my attendance at a liberal state university, had given him my name and number.

That campus ministry, its members, and the church most of them attended were tricky. On the one hand, it was all very hip and cool. These people seemed to have a fresh, new understanding of God. The student-leader was an attractive, enthusiastic, outgoing guy. His girlfriend seemed too good to be true: a former beauty queen on the university's cheerleading squad, sweet and kind to everyone she met. The weeknight meetings included a legit band full of dudes with microphones, guitars, and drums who seemed hand-picked to fill Hollywood roles: the comedian, the heartthrob, the rebel. Everyone called themselves "nondenominational" and "free," and, on Sunday afternoons, they cleared out the church's folding chairs after the service to turn the sanctuary into a full-sized basketball court. More than God as Judge, this group focused on God as Father and talked about Jesus as if he were sitting right next to me, hoping to be friends with the drummer and talking about who had won the game last week.

It was all very fun and felt very good, but some things still didn't make sense. No matter how they labeled themselves, no matter what kind of vibe they created, when the exterior was stripped away they still believed in the fundamentals of evangelical Christianity. And so, that same semester, when I enrolled in "Understanding the Bible" to fulfill our public university's religious studies requirement, my new friends were not pleased.

"It's more like '*Mis*-Understanding the Bible,'" one said.

"Yeah, it's *academic*," another person piped in. "You won't actually learn anything about the Bible."

"Don't worry. Other people here have made the mistake of enrolling in that class. You can still drop it."

But I insisted then, as I do now, that anyone with strong enough faith in her religion mustn't feel threatened by different ideas and continued in the class. And my friends were right: it *was* academic. It was educational. I learned some basic facts, information available to anyone who has curiosity and the Internet. We learned about the canonization process, for example: who decided what texts belonged in the Bible, when they decided, and how. It was the first time I heard an explanation other than "Because God said." You can imagine my surprise when I learned texts existed that *didn't* make the cut. In addition to studying the Bible, we read the gospels of Mary Magdalene, Thomas, and Judas.

I. Was. Shocked.

It was during this semester that I considered for the first time what it might mean if the Bible wasn't written by a single author. That, perhaps, the canonization process wasn't so divinely inspired after all. That some of those men may have had an agenda or two they wanted to push. I began to see that we had some awfully convenient cultural exceptions to what the Bible says about salvation, owning slaves, and the role of women, for example.

And so, like the questioning of an afterlife, my questioning of the Bible's divinity gave me newfound bravery. I took my questions to the campus ministry group, whose leaders often had canned answers with circular reasoning:

"How do we know about God?"

"Through the Bible."

"But how do we know the Bible is God's word?"

"Because it says it is."

They quoted the same verses I'd been hearing since childhood to answer my questions, which, for someone doubting the authority of the Bible, wasn't as effective as it used to be. Which is to say, not at all. For a while, I didn't push much further—didn't voice my frustration or doubt. The campus ministry group was fun, happy, and, well . . . that cute drummer. But a moment of clear illumination occurred when, through the group, I signed up to help international students "practice English," which, we were told, was actually a cover for our true mission: to tell them about Jesus. I was matched up with a French student, an intelligent young woman who was raised Catholic, now identified as an atheist, and had little patience for my fuzzy assurances about God.

"Look at the Bible," I said to her, practicing a line from C. S. Lewis's popular "trilemma" logic the campus ministry group had taught me.

"Jesus said he is the son of God. So the only three options of what this could mean is that he's a liar, lunatic, or Lord," I told her.

"Did Jesus write the Bible? Is it his firsthand account?"

"Well, no."

"Then those aren't the only three options," she replied. "What if he never actually said this? What if someone else *said* he said it? Why are you telling me there are only three options?"

I didn't know. I hadn't thought of that. And what's more, more than just "not knowing," I was intensely aware of a reflexive desire I had to tell her, "Hang tight a minute while I go ask my ministry leader how to answer your question," because this meant I wasn't thinking for myself.

I liked my new French friend. I respected her. I valued her as a person, not just an international student who needed to be saved. And from that moment on, I did not want to rely on any religious system to tell me how and what to think.

Without a fear of hell, without assurance that the Bible was a divine source of Truth, without the need to insist anything about God, I felt absolutely relieved to cast aside everything else I had been told and finally think for myself, not so much knitting a new sweater but examining the tools other people use to do so.

I took this idea of thinking for myself seriously, not just dropping out of church but also dropping out of college altogether by the fourth semester. I moved across the country. I worked as a flight attendant and met people from all over the world; I traveled and explored pavilions, cathedrals, basilicas. I visited India, where I was instructed to remove my shoes before entering a Jain temple, whose leaders taught me to respect the life of the insects crawling across the floor, and then, upon leaving, I watched as these same people literally stepped over bodies of the homeless outside the temple. Not much about *any* religion made sense. Finally, several years after those early college days, despite feeling the most alienated I'd ever been from my friends and family, I also felt most awake and alive and fulfilled by dropping any consideration of the supernatural.

In a culture where belief is the assumed default, much of a nonbeliever's time involves the negative: explaining what she's *not*, what she *doesn't* believe. But I can also tell you what I do believe. In a word, I believe in life. Its origins are a mystery to me, its end is inevitable, but the experience is incredible and I never want to take it for granted. I believe that belief is personal and dynamic and based on the experience of life. That experience, conscience, and reason are the best guides for belief. I believe that bringing the supernatural into politics, social movements, morality, purpose, and meaning is dangerous and even unethical. That, ultimately, action matters; creed doesn't.

I exist now with ideas that fill me with hope, purpose, and gratitude, that guide my actions and have nothing to do with the supernatural. Despite my fear of losing meaningful relationships with people who are religious, I've found that, ironically, a person's "religious status" is somewhat superficial: those relationships from the past that relied solely on having the same religious language and identity have fallen off long ago, while the relationships built on a deep respect and love for who we are individually have remained strong, no matter what the differences are in our beliefs. The legacy of kindness I used to describe my extended family? It's not because they are religious. It's because they are, in fact, kind.

I accept now that there are no absolute answers to those existential questions and that the journey takes place in the asking. The positive, concrete things religion offers—ceremony, community, service, comfort, reflection—these things are possible on a temporal level, without motivation from the divine. Even the consistent human desire for God's existence is explained to me by breakthroughs in psychology and science.

My current ideas and criticisms aside, I'm also a realist: religious institutions across this increasingly connected world aren't going anywhere soon and, for as many of us who are leaving religion, there are others joining. The value of reflecting on my upbringing and deconversion in my role as a parent is enhanced by appreciating religion for how personal and complicated it is. In any loss, whether it's been literal or abstract, I've found comfort using the Kübler-Ross model to help me label and understand my range of emotions. Anyone familiar with this popular and controversial "breakdown" of grief knows that the five stages—denial, anger, bargaining, depression, and acceptance—serve as flexible, overlapping categories, not necessarily experienced in order or even in full. But I do see how my journey out of religion fits into this model.

Those first experiences of doubt and the backtracking that followed, the pulling of the threads and the attempts to mend, felt much like denial: denial that those I trusted most could be wrong, that my faith was misguided, that I didn't belong in the same category as family and friends. I lived with an intuitive ache that seemed to be a manifestation of cognitive dissonance, the mental stress or discomfort experienced by an individual who holds two or more contradictory beliefs, ideas, or values at the same time or is confronted by new information that conflicts with existing beliefs, ideas, or values.

The next stage in the model, anger, is one where many apostates may find themselves stuck. Atheists don't have a reputation for being "angry" for nothing. I've witnessed many people over the years lose religion and feel as though the proverbial scales have fallen from their eyes, proceeding to ridicule, debate, or harass any believer in their paths. I can understand the anger: there are long-standing, seemingly indestructible myths prevalent in our culture that nonbelievers must have no moral compass or hope or are unable to experience awe and wonder—are not, in other words, fully human. An avid reader, I consider the influences in literature alone: classics such as Dostoevsky's novel *The Brothers Karamazov* and Flannery

O'Connor's short story "A Good Man Is Hard to Find" warn that nonbelievers are dangerous. Anyone would be angry, having to prove themselves constantly against such myths.

The bargaining tactic that I clung to for so long could be described as hypocrisy: claiming to have standards or beliefs to which one's own behavior does not conform. For many years after I left home, I went to church, used the language, attended Bible studies, even led a youth group, all while wildly doubting and living in a way that wasn't consistent with this religious self. These were times I also considered Pascal's Wager, a bargaining tactic that figures even if a person doesn't really believe, she can pretend she does, *just in case.*

Depression, the next-to-last stage, is as distressing as one would expect. Though I traded fear for freedom, I also traded acceptance for loneliness. When I was a child, I would look at visitors in church and wonder: *Are they hearing this? Is God speaking to them now? Will they accept and believe?* Now, as a nonbeliever in a world full of religious vernacular, where people discuss their prayers, blessings, and judgments loquaciously, when I am able to replace my irritation with grace, I'm left feeling, at best, unseen, unknown. And worse, before I found ways to fill the emptiness left by losing religion, having no spiritual education other than what was taught in fundamental churches, I did feel empty for a time. Cold and exposed. No answers, no ideas, no hope.

All of these stages—denial, anger, bargaining, depression—as uncomfortable and painful as they are, are tempting to stay in rather than face the unknown. But my children have nudged me to ease into a place of acceptance, of both what has been lost and what we can find together. What becomes another chapter in the story of losing my religion was first inspired that night, years ago, over spaghetti: *Who is God?*

That our sense of purpose, morality, and connectedness to others is not just possible but also much more meaningful when we're empowered to find those answers ourselves is the message I want to offer to my children during the brief time they are under my guidance. With time and maturity, everyone eventually constructs a highly personalized philosophy of life, whether it's religious or secular. It's not my job to do it for anyone else. As poet Kahlil Gibran writes of children, "You may give them your love but not your thoughts, / For they have their own thoughts. / You may house their bodies but not their souls, / For their souls dwell in the house of tomorrow, / which you cannot visit, not even in your dreams."[4]

Ironically, having children is learning to let them go. From the moment they are conceived, they're on an inevitable trajectory to grow as individuals with their own inherent worth, ability to reason, and capacity to form a philosophy of life. I want to foster that capacity as honestly as I can. The key now, after coming to peace with my own experience and power of my own influence, is balancing the reality that I'm only one in a sea of voices that will offer other options along the way.

2

RELIGIOUS
EDUCATION

Education is not the filling of a pail, but the lighting of a fire.

—William Butler Yeats

It's been more than ten years now, but I still remember the first thing a close family member asked me when I told her about my new boyfriend, Chris, the man who would become my husband. I was so excited when I called her up, overwhelmed with happiness and hope the way people are when they're falling in love, tripping over my words to tell her about him: *He's funny and smart and kind and fun.*

"Is he a Christian?" she asked.

In a moment, the air was gone.

Of course, to most Christians—to most people of faith—this is a fair question. She, a Christian, was assuming that I was still Christian, and it's easier to be in a relationship with someone who shares the same religion. I'm not saying it's right, or better, or desirable; I'm just saying it's easier. That, and, as females raised in the evangelical tradition, we'd both grown up with a particular Bible verse from 2 Corinthians as our guide to dating: *Do not be yoked together with unbelievers.*

"Uh . . . no," I stammered, *not* lying to my family for the first time about a boyfriend's religious status. Several men I'd dated as a young adult were *not* Christian, something I skirted around with my family until this point. But this time was different. I'll admit, perhaps, that the strength of my infatuation with him played a part in this newfound bravery, but mostly it was just Chris himself. I had dated nonbelievers before, and although they'd been intelligent and interesting, when the topic of religion came up they'd also been antagonistic, abrasive, even belligerent. Although I agreed with them about many philosophical points, the derision they aimed toward religion, a sacred subject for so many people I loved, made me wonder if I would ever really fit in as a "none" in the religious category. As if the old stereotypes I'd been taught about atheists weren't enough, some of the men I'd dated themselves made me wary of being identified as a nonbeliever.

Chris, however, skeptical and doubting since he was very young, an atheist since adolescence, has only been gracious, patient, and understanding toward religion since I've known him. He is absolutely uninterested in making his views known to others and absolutely confident and secure in them when pressed to do so. This was inspiring to me; this was someone who helped me understand that my identity as a nonbeliever was nothing to be ashamed of.

So, that question: *Is he a Christian?* This time, I would tell the truth. This time, I would be brave.

"He was raised in a Christian family . . . ?" I said weakly, hoping to bridge a very large gap. *Remember, be brave!* "But, no, he's not really anything now, himself."

Not really anything. This meager summation was my description for the man who would go on to be the single most influential person in my life. *Not really anything.* It was the closest I've come to telling anyone in my family what was implied: *and neither am I.*

Through our whirlwind courtship and marriage, it was clear to my religious family and friends that he was in my life, and theirs, to stay. We slipped into what Phil Zuckerman describes in his book *Living the Secular Life* as a religious "don't ask, don't tell" approach.[1] I find that it's just as well, really, as the easier it becomes for me to express what I *don't* believe, the more difficult it is for me to articulate what I do.

Put two peaceful nonbelievers in a household together, and you just don't hear much religious language—not the kind that filled the home when I was growing up. We both have contemplative practices, but for the most part they are quiet and private. After our initial discovery that we had more in common than not regarding religion and belief, for several years the topic rarely came up again.

This explains our surprise that night over dinner when our son asked, "Who is God?"

I grew up in a household in which the word *God* was said aloud regularly and with ease. Through prayers, struggles, joys, conversations, the word slipped off the tongue like breath. "Dear God" began our requests; "It's part of God's plan" answered the problem; "God made it that way" explained the unknown.

But this was now *my* little dwelling, not that of my parents, and the word *God* so rarely, if ever, had been spoken aloud in our home (at least without the word *dammit* following) that it was as though my son had asked his question through a bullhorn.

Of course, this was in our home, the one place I find relief from our culture's consumer version of Christianity. I'm used to the public spaces, where people advertise religion like it's a sports team or soda brand. I'm used to scrolling through my Facebook feed, reading a bumper sticker or billboard, scanning the radio, or listening to surface-y conversation and hearing the word *God* thrown out there so casually that I'd feel sorry for him if I thought he existed. I recently scrolled by an online header, "4 Things God Wants U to Know," sandwiched between an article on eating more fruit and an advertisement for wicking yoga pants. If this isn't using the word in vain, I don't know what is.

No matter what I share, or don't share, with my children, the way religion permeates our world is almost as inconspicuous as the air we breathe. They hear it in the Pledge of Allegiance, read it on currency, see it along the highway like litter. In more intimate settings, they absorb it through discussions on the playground, through their grandmother's stories, through nighttime whispers with their cousins.

Raising children in a culture that nonchalantly evokes the sacred in our vernacular means it's a question of when, not if, they begin to ask these questions. On this particular day, our son had spent the day with his grandmother.

"Did you say God?" I asked, to make sure I had heard correctly (and to buy some time).

"Yeah," he said. "Grandma says God is everywhere."

Chris and I looked at one another. *Is this happening already?* Although my mom had raised her own children in an evangelical environment, her beliefs have clearly evolved in the time I'd left home, gone through university, and started a family of my own. Through those years, she and I spent lots of time together, and she rarely brought up her faith.

Still, the reactive nature of my annoyance suggests that I had been expecting this. I was quick to clarify what I wish someone had for me, not just in matters of faith but in all kinds of things: just because a grown-up says so, doesn't mean It Is.

"Well, some people say God is everywhere," I began. Luke looked at his father.

"Do you say that, Daddy?"

"Um . . ." Chris struggled, and I could offer no help. I was just as curious as Luke. "No," he finally said. "I am one of those people who does not say it."

Luke looked at me. "Do you say it?"

Now I was the one shifting in my chair as Chris looked just as inquisitively at me.

"Um . . . actually, I'm a person who doesn't know what I say."

Luke considered these answers and must have remembered a conversation he had with Chris earlier that day about germs.

"Well, if God *is* everywhere, is he like bacteria?"

Considering what concrete, literal thinkers children are, God as bacteria is as good a definition as any. Notice, though, that Chris and I didn't actually answer the question, *Who is God?*

How does one answer that question for a child when adults rarely agree upon an answer for themselves? Who *is* God? Fewer and fewer people, even in the Christian tradition, still believe God is a bearded man in the sky, dressing in robes and bowling for thunder. Even so, the common understanding of God as being incorporeal, infinite, timeless, in addition to ways I've heard God defined—as "love," "goodness," or "creation"—are abstractions that are literally developmentally impossible for a child to comprehend. It's not until adolescence that a person is able to begin such abstract thinking, and so God, to a child, *must* be understood concretely. This is where Greg Epstein's observation in *Good without God* makes sense to me:

that "What do you believe *about* God?" is a more meaningful question than "Do you believe in God?"

Religious institutions' lack of acknowledgment in this basic understanding of child development is maddening to me, but never mind that I'd rather no one talk about their version of God with my children. I'll say it now and move on, lest I plump the stereotype of the angry atheist: I feel a deep frustration, to put it diplomatically, that belief in the supernatural is the default position in our culture, shifting the burden of proof for unfalsifiable claims away from the people making them. And to add to this frustration, must I explain the supernatural, abstract concepts to my kids, these little wide-eyed, naive, trusting creatures who are so desperate to please, who trust everything I say?

Yes. Yes, I must. In a way that is compassionate and understanding and kind. And talk is cheap: I must model it, too. That's the reality we live in. I can talk about my frustrations and wishes all I want, but the small corner of the universe that makes up our world is a predominantly English-speaking country with roots in the Christian tradition (despite its founding in religious freedom).

As such, the Jesus question popped up shortly after the God question, but at least we had something concrete to work with.

One afternoon, Chris took our preschoolers out on an errand to the hardware store. It was December in the Midwest, which meant the local store had a nativity scene set up in Lawn and Garden. After fondling several of the knickknacks displayed at eye level in the center aisle, they passed by the intriguing little religious statues. They inspected the animals and stable and shepherds, which seemed to make sense to them, and then stopped short:

"What's that baby doing there?" one of them asked.

Chris immediately felt self-conscious in the crowded, bustling store. Having rambunctious twin preschoolers out in public attracts attention, no matter what questions they ask, and already he was aware of people staring, some with smiles, others grimaces. He tried to hustle the kids along and said, in that sweet tone parents use in public, more for the other adults than their children, "That's the little baby Jesus."

"WHO THE HECK IS BABY JESUS?!?"

Sure, we lived in a liberal university town, but this was a hardware store in Kansas, after all, and at this point Chris was uncharacteristically flustered.

Feeling all eyes on him, he hustled right out of the store and into the parking lot, where he could explain things in the privacy of the family automobile. Chris did what he does well, much better than I do: spoke only to the questions they asked and to nothing they didn't.

"Some people say the human son of God, a baby named Jesus, was born a long time ago. People who believe this say Christmas is his birthday."

The boys felt like old pros a few weeks later when they saw the nativity again at their grandparents' Episcopal church, the church my husband calls "Catholic-lite." We had returned to Chris's hometown for the holidays and decided to take part in his family's tradition of attending midnight mass. As part of the service, the children were asked to bring stuffed animals to the scene and lay it by the manger. (To be returned at the service's conclusion, rest assured.)

It was my first time back to church in a long time, and I found the service to be refreshingly generic—even neutered—compared to the evangelical services of my past. The boys took pride in their role with the stuffies, we patted ourselves on the back for exposing them to part of our culture and heritage, and gave ourselves extra points because they wore ties. It went so well, in fact, we felt confident in continuing this tradition each time we returned for Christmas. In addition to making family happy, it proved a valuable lesson on distinguishing between fact and belief. We reminded the kids often and gently that just because some people believe certain things doesn't mean others have to.

Because we lived in one of the most progressive enclaves in the Midwest, other than this little seasonal taste of religion for the kids, we went along for several years without addressing many other details. It was as though, if we pretended long enough, religion would cease to exist.

They were six years old, cruising through Wyoming, when they heard the word *devil* for the first time. We had taken two weeks to drive from Kansas to California when we moved, camping at National Parks along the way. After stopping at a point of interest, I read the placard along the road.

"That ridge is called 'Devil's Backbone,'" I said, pointing to a jagged line of rocks that rose straight up from the prairie.

"Why?" one of them asked. "What's a devil?"

It took until Nevada to answer all the questions that followed.

This sort of holidays-and-legends-only track we were on seems pretty typical for nonreligious parents coming from a religious background, but of course we recognized a major flaw in the approach on that fateful Easter weekend with family. The whole cute-little-baby-Jesus-turned-hairy-man-who-is-whipped-and-killed goes over with young children exactly how it sounds it might. At that time, the boys were nine and their little sister was four, and I was just beginning to understand that I needed to put some thought and intention into the whole religion thing. It surprises me now how little consideration I gave the approach to religion as a parent, especially considering how much consideration I gave it in my inner life.

It's a common, flawed assumption believers have that nonbelievers aren't "there yet," like belief is an inevitable destination at which they'll arrive after enough consideration or experience—at least, this is a generalization I heard over and over growing up in the church. Most nonbelievers I've met or studied put a great deal of thought into belief and, when given a chance, can very thoroughly explain their position. So, frankly, it surprises me that so many secular parents, who have clearly put much thought into both religion and parenting, take the approach I was taking: perhaps if we just ignore—or sometimes ridicule—religion, it will go away.

I understand, all too well, the fervor with which churches and parents teach their chosen religion to children, but I haven't seen many examples of religion and spirituality being taught to children in an unbiased, educational way. It's rather baffling: for better or worse, religion shapes our world just as much as other subjects—history, science, literature—and it's in our best interest, as parents who value education and critical thought, to prepare our children for ways to understand what they'll hear about belief. It seems as though we are confusing education with indoctrination, but, as Aristotle said, "It is the mark of an educated mind to be able to entertain a thought without accepting it."

I blame the problem on an unwillingness in many adults to reconcile what we "know" in our rational minds with what we "know" beneath our minds, in that deep, inner churning some people call the gut, but, really, it's boundless; I'm not talking about a spirit or soul, but a hidden consciousness somewhere between the heart and the stomach that holds the impact of our lived experiences we can't directly face. The ones that make us unwittingly clinch our fists or hold our breath or stop time when we taste a sliver of melon, hear a certain melody, or smell a trace of honeysuckle.

Had I not been raised in the Christian tradition, perhaps I'd have an easier time understanding and explaining Jesus—the man, the teacher, the radical—but it's not so easy for me to comb through the tangle of the person with the threads of the supernatural, the history, the myth. Perhaps if I hadn't known God for so long to be an all-knowing, all-powerful being willing to send someone I loved to hell or unwilling to save strangers who suffer, perhaps I could explore other concepts with my children. But I've stepped away from myself far enough that I can see the bias and unwillingness to "know" what I *know*, and it's clear to me now that someone should guide my children to find answers to their questions, but it shouldn't always be me.

I had made up my mind that it's time for "religious education," like it's a singular event that would be distinct on my kids' childhood timelines, but, of course, this is not how meaningful understanding works. Right around the time I realized religious education is an actual thing and considered my options to approach it, I realized the foundations were already being built, by a surprising source: one Mr. Rick Riordan, author of the Percy Jackson and the Olympians series.

The boys were third graders when they first brought home a Percy Jackson book, and, frankly, I was relieved, not because of the contents of the book but its thickness. We live in an ambitious, hypereducated part of the country, where parents brag about their kindergartners reading chapter books and recommend summer school when first-graders aren't doing the same. Intrinsically, I didn't doubt my children's intelligence or worry about literacy, but it seemed everyone around me was panicked when my nine-year-olds went for a Garfield comic book instead of *War and Peace*.

Soon enough, though, they were coming home with these big, thick, regal-looking hardcovers and couldn't put them down. I was so excited about their own excitement that I didn't ask or even care what the books were about. They were marked "Grade 4–8 Interest Level, Adventure and Mythology" from the school library, which was good enough for me.

I discovered a few months later on a car ride exactly how much they were learning during a family discussion on the romantic life of banana slugs. We had just moved to a redwood grove outside San Francisco, home to the

Ariolimax californicus, or California banana slug. These bright yellow slugs, some of the largest in the world, are the most popular residents of our little alpine rain forest. Our neighbors have placed a "Banana Slug Crossing" sign on the road, and my kids constructed the "Banana Slug Healing Center" for injured or tired slugs. They are everywhere underfoot, and it's not unusual to see them curled up around one another like a sunny yin-yang symbol for hours as they take their sweet time copulating.

"It says here that they're hermaphrodites," I said, reading a Wikipedia entry on my phone at a stoplight, after our kindergartner asked if her new pet slug was a boy or a girl. "That means they have girl parts *and* boy parts."

"That must be because Hermes is male and Aphrodite is female," one of the boys said, nonchalantly.

"Yep," the other agreed. "It makes sense, too, because Aphrodite is the goddess of love and Hermes is the guide to the underworld. Like a mating slug."

"How in the world do you know all this?" I asked, looking in the rearview mirror.

My eye met blank stares. *How do you* not *know all this?*

"Percy Jackson," one of them finally said.

Who is this Percy Jackson? It turns out he's the protagonist of the Olympians series, a twelve-year-old boy who discovers he's the modern-day son of the ancient Greek god Poseidon, a god I knew little about. Growing up, I had been taught that Greek mythology was a direct threat to Christianity and learned very little about it, other than that the names of the gods and goddesses are associated with heresy and evil.

I was suddenly very aware of my ignorance, but the boys were thrilled to teach me what they knew: that Poseidon is god of the sea, the one who causes earthquakes and carries a trident. They laughed when I mispronounced his name and broke it to me gently that he was originally eaten by his own father, Cronus, but was ultimately rescued by his little brother, Zeus.

What a jarring, heartbreaking, hopeful realization I had that my children were learning about things I hadn't—mythology, etymology, sociology—in ways I couldn't—with inquiry, objectivity, irreverence—no shame, fear, or ignorance to speak of. Education, as it should be.

I'll admit, even after deciding that my children should learn *about* religion, I wasn't exactly sure *what* they should learn about it. Because my position is that belief should not be taught as truth, I don't want to teach any take on belief as truth. Parents who might deride religion in front of their children without considering why so many are drawn to it need to remember that confidence and sincerity in one's journey is directly correlated with the amount of education and autonomy one has had along the way. I've had fellow nonbelievers proudly share stories of their young children, sometimes preschool age, clomping to school to inform their classmates that God Doesn't Exist. Like the young child wearing ultrahip clothes claiming to love Neil Young, the one declaring himself to be an atheist tells me more about his parents than the child.

Atheist and antitheist thinkers have influenced my beliefs, and I agree with many of their positions, but I have arrived at these conclusions in my twenties and thirties and expect them to evolve further. I'm not going to sit my nine-year-olds down with *The God Delusion* and expect them to get any more out of it than they would a religious text. No, I'm not teaching them *what* to think; it's *how* to think that I'm after.

To that end, I've realized what I intend to teach them about religion is in line with *freethought*, the philosophical viewpoint that truth should be formed on the basis of logic, reason, and empiricism rather than authority, tradition, or dogma.

Even though the word has been around for centuries, I first heard the term *freethinker* when I was looking for books on parenting without religion and found Dale McGowan's *Raising Freethinkers*. I immediately pictured a barefoot hippie girl, strumming a guitar with a crown of wildflowers in her long hair, circa 1969. Much to my surprise, I learned the concept of freethought emerged toward the end of the seventeenth century, landmarked by Dominican monk Giordano Bruno's 1600 execution by the Inquisition for heresy. The term itself gained understanding and usage in England through the next century and spread throughout Europe and the United States, where the Freethought movement was organized as the Free Press Association in 1827, when blasphemy was still a crime. In the late 1800s, or the "Golden Age" for freethinkers, the group reorganized several times, under new names and leaders, and advocated for racial, sexual, and social equality before the members disbanded and integrated into mainstream liberal churches.

The legacy and philosophy of freethought provided both inspiration and a loose framework I needed to begin this religious education business.

Between my interest in freethinking and the boys' interest in Greek mythology, I felt like we had a starting point. To someone who doesn't have such an intense, personal history with religion, studying Greek gods and myths as our primer may seem so obvious or trite as to be cliché. But when the kids sincerely wondered if people in present-day Greece believe in the wild stories of the Greek gods the way Americans believe in the wild stories of the Christian God, I realized that any wild story has equal plausibility to a child. We might as well start with the earlier ones and work our way forward. And it was a relief to me to have fun exploring origins, deities, rewards, punishments, and immortality in a way that wouldn't step on anyone's toes or open the carousel for all my personal baggage.

"Goddammit, you guys, we're gonna be late for church!"

My first attempt at taking religious education public wasn't going as planned. After months of studying and discussing some pretty horrific Greek legends, the kids were ready for modern religion. I didn't realize this journey would bring me back to church, but there I was, trying to herd cats to the local Unitarian Universalist Fellowship. The UUF we were visiting is careful to distinguish themselves as a *fellowship*—a friendly association—and not a *church*—a place for Christian worship—which makes sense considering their purpose and the definitions. But the word *fellowship*, for me, still conjures up the idea of people calling one another "brother" and "sister" and discussing Jesus over coffee and pie.

The only association with Unitarianism I'd had prior to this was celebrity weddings, as reported in *People* magazine. I certainly didn't expect that it would be cause for me to bribe my family of heathens to put on their shoes and slink into the congregation late on a Sunday morning. But I confess: as a nonbeliever with a believer's past, it was both reassuring and disconcerting to know that we were doing the exact same thing as many other families across the county.

So why was I doing this? That's what several of our nonreligious friends wanted to know when I told them what we were up to, especially those with similar misgivings about the Unitarian tradition. "I thought you were even more of an atheist than me," one of my friends said. "Isn't it still *church*?" And another: "So are Birkenstocks optional or required?"

I knew "Unitarian" is cause for alarm to conservative Christians. (Like "ecumenical," a word I asked a friend about back in my college days: "You just run as far away from that as possible," she said. "It's tricks and lies to make everyone think whatever they want to believe is OK.") But now I realized that nonreligious people give it pushback, too.

I decided to go straight to the source and spent hours on the UU website reading about their history, their principles, and, most important, their take on religious education. Yes, both Unitarianism and Universalism (which were separate entities until 1961) had their roots in Christianity, but those roots were severed and replanted in the soil of skepticism, heresy, and doubt. They take pride in the label *heretic*, as Mark Harris explains in writing on UU history: "*heresy*, in Greek, means *choice*." One of the first Unitarian preachers, Francis David, declared, "We need not think alike to love alike."

Today, the Universalist Unitarian Association describes itself as people congregating to support "the free and responsible search for truth and meaning," and it includes members from Western and Eastern traditions as well as atheists, agnostics, and secular humanists. I read that many current newcomers find themselves at a UU fellowship specifically for the religious education program. They are often nonreligious parents from religious backgrounds looking for an unbiased way to expose their kids to religion.

Perfect.

The only problem, I discovered, is that kids going to Unitarian fellowship are the same as kids going to Catholic mass or Jewish synagogue or Muslim mosque.

"Do we *have* to go?"

"Why??"

"Can't we invite our friends???"

I was tempted to launch into a "When I was your age . . ." lecture, but instead, I said this: "Learning about religion is like your piano lessons: it's something that will be valuable to you as you get older, like math, science, and literature, but they don't teach it at school. Like music, religion has its own language that lots of people speak, and we think it's important that you understand a bit of what they're saying."

Or something like that. Anyway, that's what I like to think I said.

When we got to the building, an unassuming structure on the corner of a residential block, the obvious distinguishing feature was the "Unitarian Fellowship" lettering in a brown, distinctly 1970s shagadelic font. A gentle-but-competent-looking woman, Cindy, smiled at us from the entrance, introduced herself, and before I knew it, all five of us were wearing name tags that the kids had decorated with insect stickers. The first people we met were a family with children close to ours in age.

"We're here to undo some damage done by an evangelical babysitter," the father explained.

We settled into a row of padded chairs three-quarters of the way back, where I was able to let go of the breath I'd been holding, look around, and make sense of my surroundings.

At first glance, it *looked* like church. There were dark, somber-looking hymnals on every other seat, rows of mostly silver-haired heads in front of me, and an elevated platform in the front that contained what someone might call a lectern. Sunlight flooded the dark-wood arch-braced roof, candles flickered along the perimeter, and a sleek piano took up the front left corner.

But as the moments passed, I realized how very different one thing was, a difference that let me relax my shoulders, feel the chair underneath me, and lower an invisible shield I hadn't realized I'd raised.

There was no mention of God. There was no talk of prayer, blessings, miracles, salvation, or sin. There were no crosses, no stars, no doves, no fish. Those dark hymnals contained songs like "Come, Come, Whoever You Are" and "Lean on Me." The big metal symbol in the front of the room, I learned, was a chalice set inside two interlocking circles. Some-one lit a candle in the chalice, which, in typical UU fashion, can represent whatever one chooses for it: some common interpretations are that it's the light of reason, the warmth of community, the flame of hope. People in the congregation stood up and shared their "joys and sorrows." The children were asked to carry donations of food and products to the front, listened to a story about emptying a bowl of rice so that it may be refilled, and then left for their classes while we sang "Go now in peace / let the spirit of love surround you." The reverend gave a philosophical talk on striking a balance between holding onto hope and letting go of fear, and we closed with "Let It Be."

For the first time in a long time, it felt really good to go to church. Except it's not church. But I also can't quite bring myself to say "fellowship."

I said we were checking out the fellowship for the kids, but I've probably gotten more out of it than they have. They would rather stay with the adults when the children are dismissed, as our service intrigues and quiets them: they're drawn to the stillness of the sanctuary, the glow of candles, the sound of music that draws like moths to a flame. For now, my children report that their favorite parts are: (1) snacks in the social hall after class, (2) climbing the tree out front, and (3) bringing other "Diablos," friends from their pre-church indoor soccer team who sometimes join us, a handful of boys wearing bright red "Diablos" jerseys, ready for some religious education.

Ironically, they started in during the "Christianity" series.

"What'd you learn?" I asked one Sunday.

"So Jesus was, like, this really generous guy, and he asked these brothers to join him selling fish. He said to them, 'You're gonna make *so much money.*'"

I've loosened up since first deciding to be proactive about religious education. The most important part of the decision was realizing the need to talk about it in the first place. Our attendance at the UUF has been somewhat sporadic, and I don't push it when the boys are dead set against going. Because of her personality and age, our daughter gets the most out of it right now, and sometimes she and I will go together while Chris and the boys go on a bike ride or hit the beach.

Don't I know this? Real education doesn't come from the classroom, or textbook, or lectures, anyway. Especially now that I'm willing to confront my biases and acknowledge my limitations, education comes from spontaneous discussions in the car and around the dinner table and, of course, in the actions modeled.

Chris, with his calm, rational approach to things, has never been upset when someone talks to the kids about religion. "It gives them a reason to ask questions," he said.

It's true. Even after the Easter service with their cousins that I so regret, we talked about Christianity, God, and religion for almost the entire six-hour car ride home. I've come to accept that firm believers will want to talk to my kids, especially if issues of salvation are involved, as they often are. As long as no one tries to hide it from me or insists the kids keep it a secret, I now trust the process.

I've been insisting that belief is a dynamic, ongoing journey; this is why I think teaching it any other way is so harmful. So what I can do now is talk about my own curiosities and questions with the kids, my own wonders and theories, doubts and frustrations. I'm thrilled now to know which one of them currently believes in a god (or several), which one thinks there's an afterlife, which one believes in prayer. Sometimes their minds change *while* they're answering the question. This, I think, captures the difference between education and indoctrination: education lets them know what *some people* think and believe, and it lets them try out the ideas. Indoctrination tells them *what* to think and believe, stifling the possibility that they can discover what makes sense for themselves.

And as a parent, I'm constantly reminded of the quote by Robert Heinlein, another Midwesterner-turned-Californian, a nonconformist who used writing to explore the ways religion influences society: "When one teaches, two learn."

INTERLUDE: BOSTON

I was twenty years old, working as a flight attendant out of Logan airport, and living in a suburb of Boston when I decided to try an experiment. By this point, I was full of doubt over my religion. I'd been through three semesters of college, woven in and out of churches and groups, left my roots behind in the Midwest, and went looking for new soil out east. Working and traveling, I would still tell anyone who asked that I was a Christian, a vestigial reaction from my past. The angst over my hypocrisy and deception was eating away at me even more than the loneliness caused by my doubt.

It was, indeed, a lonely time. I didn't have a home; I spent more time in planes, airports, and hotels than I did in my own bedroom, which was constructed with curtains and a mattress in the basement of a friend's house. I didn't have any stable relationships; I lived for the high of meeting new people, having perfected chameleon-like identity changes depending on their needs and then slipping out of their lives as quickly as I slipped in. I had no semblance of a routine or schedule; the airline could call at any time, day or night, and I had to be ready to go anywhere from Anchorage to Mumbai for more than a week at a time.

I spent many of those days on call exploring the area, alone. One of my favorite places to go was Boston Square. This buzzing green space in the middle of the city, along Beacon Street and close to the Charles River, was the perfect spot to people watch, read, or just walk around and feel part of something. One day, during a haze of existential confusion, I was feeling particularly low when I walked by a grand church on Park Street. In the historic fashion I love about the city, this building was brick-sturdy and imposing, with a huge steeple that swept my eyes to the sky.

I suppose I did not have the response that the architects of this church were going for. I heard myself say, *I just don't believe in God.* While my thoughts had been flitting around this idea for a while, it was the first time I had allowed the declaration to settle front and center, bypassing all of the instructions and warnings I'd grown up with—what it meant, I finally realized, to be honest with oneself. I looked around, afraid someone, somehow, could read my thoughts. *No one has to know. It's just me and my mind, and I'm going to walk around this city, not believing, and see what happens.*

Well, of course, nothing happened. I mean, I stopped and bought a gyro from a street vendor and watched some handicapped pigeons pilfer food at the base of Brewer Fountain, but that's about it. Incredibly anticlimactic. Having grown up with this God who was so invested in my inner life—what my thoughts were, who I loved, when I prayed—I was expecting for the sky to darken or a plane to crash into the harbor. Or, at least, that I would trip and lose my sandwich to the birds.

No, nothing big, sudden, or dramatic took place, which probably wouldn't surprise anyone but those of us brought up in a fundamentalist faith. What unfolded instead, though, may have been worse. Because when a person is told from the time before she can even think for herself that God is the only source for such essential issues of being as morality, transcendence, and purpose, you can imagine what sort of slow, dull ache sets in when she *does* begin to think for herself and realizes that she, in fact, does not believe God exists.

What struck me that night as I climbed onto my mattress in the basement—what was both comforting and confusing—was that I had just rejected a story I've been told from the beginning that explained every iota of my being, and yet . . . *I was still the same person.* I still knew how to love and be loved; I was still overcome by and grateful for the mystery and beauty of life; I still had a desire to be and do good. All of these things that I had been told for so long were dependent on my belief in God were still right there. I felt I had just taken a big risk—perhaps that I had traded my soul for my mind—and came out intact. Better than intact: harmonious. No trade-offs or dissonance required.

But still, in the many years it took me to say out loud what I'd decided so quietly that day, I had a lot to work out in my mind. If God wasn't, in fact, the source for all love, joy, meaning, purpose, and sense of right and wrong contained within me, then what was? What history, ideas, and language could I access to understand these things? And how can I offer something different to my children?

3

MORALITY

How much more precious is a little humanity than all the rules in the world.

—Jean Piaget

The summer before I started eighth grade, my family moved to a new town. I *really* didn't want to go. It wasn't moving itself; we'd already moved almost every year of my life before this, and I always thought of it as an adventure, with different faces and bare houses promising possibility and a fresh start. What was killing me was where we were going. It was only an hour away, but it might as well have been another universe to my thirteen-year-old self. We'd been living in a college town, where my older brothers went to university, and it felt big, exciting, diverse. Families were more transient, as ours had been. I made good friends during the year we lived there, including one whose parents offered to let me stay and live with them through high school. I'm not sure my mom even *remotely* considered this a possibility. She wanted me to be happy—it must have been hard for her to see me so miserable—but she couldn't bear to let me go and grow up somewhere else.

The thing I hated most about this new town was the monotony. It was a small town, a place that thrives on uniformity, and I just never felt like I fit in. Most of my new classmates had lived in the same house all their lives; they had memories together from kindergarten. Everyone knew the names of everyone else's siblings, parents, and grandparents. There were literal train tracks that divided the town, and our new house was most definitely on the wrong side. I felt like an outsider the moment we arrived, and identities cultivated in adolescence stick with us a long time.

I spent most of that summer alone, exploring on my bike. I rode to what would be my new school and stood in front of it, assessing. One of those days, the tears came. I can still feel the pain in my chest now, a pain I had never felt before that day. I was sad, yes, about moving and missing my friends and having to give up a life I'd imagined to be so much better. But I'd been feeling that way all summer. This time, the pain felt bigger, deeper than anything I'd experienced, and I had a distinct thought: *People all over the word have felt this way.*

I was surprised by this thought—where did it come from?—but it was so luminous, it shone a light on everything I did for quite some time. It had the ability to make me feel better and worse. When I laughed. When I cried. When I got hungry. When I got angry. When I felt lonely. When I felt loved. *People all over the world have felt this way.*

After a while, the brightness of this revelation dimmed down and settled into more of a constant, tiny glow that I assume will remain within my consciousness until I take my last breath. *People all over the world have felt this way.* And I didn't know it then—I'm only really beginning to understand now—but this experience became the foundation for an understanding of morality that has stayed with me long after I left religion.

I've been thinking about ways to articulate what shapes my moral code as my children get older, though, in retrospect, I should have been doing this as soon as they asked their first "Why?" Of all the existential foundations I had been taught as a child that were entirely dependent on God, perhaps the one most in need of a philosophical rehaul for me, the one most distorted by a religious upbringing, was my understanding of right and wrong. Even though a 2014 Pew Research Poll shows that 53 percent of Americans assert that belief in God is essential to morality, when I dropped my belief in God I found myself to be a walking embodiment of the problems with this assertion and had a lot to work out.[1]

If one's moral instruction is dependent on specific rules, texts, or authority, it will only be as strong as her faith in those things. Losing my religion did not, as I'd been warned for so long, cause me to lose my desire to be and do good. What I did lose was my basis for understanding *what it means* to be and do good. I moved through most of my twenties using only intuition as my guide, but in the same way it does for most issues, being a parent forces me to reflect more directly on a question that is both extremely simple and incredibly complicated: What is the right thing to do?

Being able to answer this question has taken a lot of unpacking for me, a lot of unfolding instructions and rules, shaking, airing out, culling. And of course, now that I have children of my own, I have some repacking to do, something I can offer to them as one of their first teachers. After all, morality requires education: even those who agree we are born with an evolutionarily based, innate understanding of right and wrong go on to say that circumstance, modeling, and instruction further shape it. And for a long time, the church has had a monopoly on morality. It's not hard to understand why, either. Even though I don't agree that using religion is necessary—or even right—for moral education, it would admittedly be so much easier to sit God-fearing children down with a list of ten hard-and-fast commandments (a handy one being *honor thy father and mother*) and be done with it rather than what I'm doing now, which is, well . . . what *am* I doing now? How am I prioritizing and fostering the ability for my children to develop a sustainable moral code, independent of religious belief?

I begin by thinking back to my own childhood, the things I was taught about right and wrong. When I think about my own lessons in morality, I think of lots of rules, given by figures of assumed authority: instructions at school, directives from my dad, commandments at church. For the most part, I feared this authority, and this fear made me follow the rules. I was terrified of getting into trouble in a Texas elementary school, where the principal still used corporal punishment via "swats" delivered by a wooden board. I was afraid of my dad's temper, as he modeled the same patriarchal, authoritarian framework he had grown up with as a child. I was eager to please the adults at church, who told me that following God's rules would save me from burning in hell for eternity.

This type of behavior-through-fear model of morality—following rules given to you by someone else—runs through my mind, in a sort of twisted spiral, like a double helix or barber's pole. But running alongside it, parallel in my mind, is another helix, another revolving spiral of moral deliberation, and this one was shaped by my mother. My mother was, ultimately, my real-life model of morality in action, the most influential and least authoritative figure in my life. She was a believer, yes, and by orchestrating my participation in Christianity, sending me off to school, and living under the same roof as my father, she implicitly enforced their rules. But on her own, she is a gentle, nonconfrontational, nonconforming person with an independent streak, which meant, at home when my dad wasn't around, we didn't have many strict guidelines. I remember my mother getting upset and reprimanding us only when we disobeyed her one general rule, which wasn't really a rule as much as a *way*: be kind to others. Be kind to your sisters and brothers, be kind to your neighbors, be kind to your classmates, be kind to strangers, be kind to parents. Be kind, be kind, be kind. Especially when you don't feel like being kind.

Until adolescence, I was a good kid. I didn't really question any of the rules. I memorized them and, for the most part, followed them. I still remember the shame I felt when I got into trouble—for belching on command at school to make my classmates laugh when we had a substitute teacher, exclaiming "Oh, my Lord!" once in front of my parents at my tenth birthday party, having to change my shorts at Bible Camp because they were too short—these transgressions may seem slight, but I was taught that God does not discriminate among sin, with memorized Bible verses to back it up: *For whosoever shall keep the whole law, and yet offend in one point, he is guilty of all.*[2] Even the smallest screw-ups had me convinced of my wickedness; I was one of the children who went up to the altar after a service to weep for my sins and ask for forgiveness.

But around junior high—around the time an intense level of suffering brought awareness of my universal connection with humanity—I realized that the long list of rules I'd memorized, which I'd understood to be absolute, were highly subjective. I studied all of the Christian influences around me, all of the people I thought to be "good," and noticed each person seemed to have their own lines of what was okay and what wasn't, which meant even belief in God didn't provide absolutes.

By high school, I was stereotypically rebellious. So many of the rules just didn't make sense. I would break one and then break another, with logic that figured, if all sin is equal in the eyes of God and I'd already let him down by swearing and piercing my ears, I might as well lie to my parents, sneak out of the house, and drink myself into a stupor after Friday night football games. The rules I followed and broke were in constant flux, regularly dependent on Sunday morning forgiveness to ease my Saturday night conscience. That's the thing about outsourcing morality: I was holding myself accountable to an authority I was rapidly beginning to doubt. But still, because of that small glow in my consciousness—*people all over the world have felt this way*—this whisper of instruction remained pertinent: *be kind to others*. I moved forward, through doubt and deconversion, with my mother's instruction as my guide, intuiting that the key to a secular moral code was contained in it, even if I wasn't sure exactly how.

When I left religion altogether, I became acutely aware of it when believers close to me, ignorant of the change in my inner life, claimed that without God people don't know right from wrong—that the godless are all murderers, liars, and thieves. That people who are religious want to be good and people who aren't religious want to be bad. Or, similarly, when loved ones said things like "Oh, he's a Christian" to clarify that the person was a good person or wouldn't do something nasty. Or "I'm a Christian," as if this were an obvious explanation for how she or he felt about complicated, subjective moral issues.

Clearly, I knew this rhetoric was incorrect. I might not be religious or believe in God, but I know right from wrong. I know how to be good. I know how not to be nasty. However, for a very long time, when pressed, I couldn't articulate *how* I knew. And this bothered me. The issue of secular morality is, perhaps, the bulkiest piece of baggage on the carousel after my flight from religion. It causes me to go out of my way to show people that a nonreligious person can also be a kind person, which, theoretically, should be a win-win. Of all axes to grind, overcompensating with kindness because of my atheism shouldn't be a problem. But as a mother raising children outside of religion, I wonder if I sometimes hold *them* to unfair standards as a reaction to my fear that we are judged for our actions, language, and behavior in a way that a religious family isn't.

I know I'm not alone: after Phil Zuckerman, a secular studies professor at Pitzer College, published his 2015 op-ed in the *Los Angeles Times*, "How Secular Family Values Stack Up," my inbox was full of excited, relieved messages from friends and colleagues linking to the piece, in which Zuckerman concludes, "Children raised without religion have no shortage of positive traits and virtues, and they ought to be warmly welcomed as a growing American demographic."[3]

This is a wonderful declaration for secular parents, one to be celebrated, but that it's a question in the first place, that we need scientific studies and data to prove our children can be "good" without religion, really demonstrates the influence of a dangerous misconception. As an apostate with insider knowledge, this kind discrimination feels so personal. I suppose this explains why an assertion that humanist chaplain Greg Epstein makes in his book *Good without God* resonates with me: that those of us with a secular moral code must think about and be able to articulate who we are and what we stand for. Otherwise, he writes, "We become a blank slate, a convenient place for religious people of all kinds to project their fears about immorality and degeneration."[4]

I picked up Epstein's book when I realized that I wanted a bit more heft behind some of the moral guidelines I was giving my children. It's one thing that I can't articulate much about secular morality to the religious crowd—I may have to leave that to people more learned than me—but it's another that I stammer and stall when thinking about how to explain it to my kids. It starts out easy enough: in the beginning, we tell our children, *Share toys. Don't hit. Say sorry.* Because we are enormous giants who can crush them in an instant, they listen. But as we've *all* matured, I've also valued and encouraged skills that were discouraged in my own childhood—critical thinking, questioning authority, and trusting intuition—which means I need some accessible ways to express complex ideas.

A suggestion that comes up often—Zuckerman refers to it in his article and Epstein writes about it in his book—is the Golden Rule: *Treat others the way you want to be treated.* And this is certainly a good place to start. My mother's emphasis on treating others with kindness is a correlation of the Golden Rule, and it's one of the few instructions from my childhood I never questioned. For a while, I felt comfortable using the Golden Rule as a guideline. It may be one of the few moral instructions we can teach in public schools without fear of lawsuits over the First Amendment or indoctrination. Without thinking twice, I often hear myself and other caretakers ask children, "How would you feel if he did that to you?"

But as my kids get older and cause me to think it through, a few more questions come up. They don't negate the impact of the Golden Rule, mind you, but they do require I find a little more depth behind it. Many people associate the Golden Rule with modern religion—as a child, I was taught to credit Jesus with the concept—but the first documented reference to the Golden Rule dates back to Confucius, who lived from 551 to 479 BCE. The story goes that a student asked him "Is there any single saying that one can act upon all day and every day?" (which is what I'm currently wondering), and Confucius told his student about *shu*, or consideration: "Never do to others what you would not like them to do to you."[5]

But for some reason, pointing to the Golden Rule alone does not seem like enough for me. For starters, it sets the bar pretty low. It's certainly a step up from "do whatever you want," but I also know that there's more to treating people well than projecting your own wants and needs onto them. What if another person wants something *different* from you? This lack of perspective can be the source of major misunderstanding and heartbreak. And it's something we can learn to navigate: studies in empathetic development show that as young as eighteen to twenty-four months old, a child is capable of *theory of mind*, which is the ability to identify that the thoughts and feelings one person has won't necessarily be the same as another.[6]

Another thing that strikes me about the Golden Rule, or its more sophisticated cousin, *empathetic reciprocity*, or, really, morality in general, is that believing the way we treat one another matters in the first place, and that it matters that we treat them well. It relies on the truth of a principle that is the closest thing I have to an absolute: that every person has an equal right to live with dignity. This is a principle I have that I didn't even *realize* I had until I took time to reflect on what values I might be modeling to my children—values that I might take for granted as obvious, even as they are foundational. As I consider morality and ethics, I realize that I need to backtrack to origin concepts of principles and values, those core beliefs that morality and ethics are based upon.

Our values—the things in life to which we ascribe worth—are the basis for shaping the rest of our lives and another component of morality that was confused by my Christian upbringing. Growing up, I had been taught and believed that God was to be valued most; human beings came second.

Therefore, if religious instruction conflicted with what was in the best interest of other people, which it sometimes did, so be it. But once I no longer believed in God, what I valued most was open for further reflection.

For someone who doesn't consider a god when prioritizing values, logic usually follows that human life is of most worth. However, what I had been taught about human nature as a Christian is fundamentally different from what I understand about human nature now. It wasn't just that human beings are flawed or imperfect; it was that human beings exist in a fundamentally deficient state without God. If this is a person's understanding of human nature, then a value system based on prioritizing human beings over all else means a value system founded in human deficiency: in "wickedness" and "sin."

What adds further misunderstanding is the difference in the way a person expresses her values when her priority is an invisible being: How does one demonstrate she values a god? A key component in my religious expression of value was "worship." If worship—extravagant admiration for or devotion to an object—is of utmost importance in expressing value, then, I was taught, those people who value human beings instead of supernatural ones must "worship" them. This is why my Christian self so misunderstood humanism: I was trained in the concept of using worship to express what I value most and assumed that if a person didn't worship a god, she must worship *something*. But what I know now is that "worship" has nothing to do with secular values, morality, and ethics. Giving something the highest value when shaping your moral code is not the same as worshipping it.

Because belief in God is so ubiquitous, usually the default position in our culture, Epstein encourages people to let go of the yes/no question *Do you believe in God?* and replace it with the question *What do you believe* about *God?*[7] In the same sense, when considering secular morality and what I've identified as a core principle—that every person has the equal right to live with dignity— I ask myself the question, "What do you believe about *people?*" Like this question, the ones my children ask about instructions for their behavior—the *why*, *how*, and *what if*—nudges me to make sense of my own childhood instructions on behavior, what has come undone since then and what still needs to be worked out. In a way, I'm traveling the same journey as them.

When in doubt, the writer in me turns to the basics of an idea by starting with its definition. But the definition of morality—*principles concerning the distinction between right and wrong or good and bad*—creates more questions. Right and wrong, good and bad: these labels are relative, and, when trying to understand the rules, my children crave absolutes. Unlike the adults from my childhood, I don't have an all-knowing being or a sacred text to measure those relative terms against, but, I figure, there's got to be some standard we can work with.

And this is where Greg Epstein helped me out. Breaking down our understanding of the word *good* in the context of morality, Epstein writes, "There is no good except between people." He uses examples around us— the sun, butterflies, lampposts, motorcycles, medicine; they are not "good" or "bad," he points out, "except insofar as they give us pleasure or pain, benefit or harm." Even the concept of a good God "would have to be one that did good things for people." After all of the battles are fought, sacrifices are made, and eternity assignments are handed out, "God's overall, long-term plan has our best interest at heart."[8]

It's people, I realized—*other people*. We are the meaning makers, truth seekers, the only species perplexed by our own existence. We determine through our shared humanity what is right and wrong, good and bad, moral and ethical. The more we explore and understand our shared humanity, which includes exploring and understanding ourselves, the more we know what is right and good. This may be a simple, obvious concept for someone without my history, but for me, it's been a revelation. I don't remember ever being told as a child that I had the ability within to distinguish right from wrong; in fact, I understood the opposite to be true, that looking within would only cause depravity. But I want to give my children something I didn't have: the confidence that their own thoughts and experiences will help them know the right thing to do. Which means, frankly, that I'm going to need to learn to embrace ambivalence, rebellion, and mistakes.

A children's book that illustrates this concept in an accessible way is one we received as a gift one Christmas, when my oldest were four. It was the book *The Three Questions*, written by Jon Muth, with a note, "based on a story by Leo Tolstoy" on the title page. In the story, a boy named Nikolai has three questions he believes are key to knowing how to be a good person: "When is the best time to do things? Who is the most important one? What is the right thing to do?" He has some animal friends—a heron, a monkey, and a dog—who offer answers with good intentions, but their suggestions are highly subjective, clearly influenced by their immediate existence and personal desires, and, he thinks, they don't seem quite right.

Nikolai decides to ask a wise, old turtle, Leo, who listens to his questions and inadvertently sees him through an adventure, which ends up teaching Nikolai that he knew the answers all along: "Remember then," Leo says, "that there is only one important time, and that time is now. The most important one is always the one you are with. And the most important thing is to do good for the one who is standing at your side."[9]

That winter, I read the story to the boys, who listened patiently, tracing the illustrations with their chubby fingers. They didn't seem particularly moved by the book; we've had it for more than six years now, and while it makes its way through the rotation, it's been nowhere as popular as *Walter the Farting Dog*. But, I, for one, was mesmerized, and the story has stayed with me since. It was one of those times my children got a lesson in something much earlier than I ever did, one of those times I learned when I thought I was teaching.

Understanding morality as something that can be articulated in succinct instructions or rules, like *The Three Questions*, is a difficult habit to break, which explains why I was so hopeful when a book promising to do so showed up on my doorstep a few days after I told my neighbor, Brian, that I've been thinking about secular morality. Brian, who describes himself as "spiritual but not religious," is a Colorado-Rocky-Mountain-Bred-Holly-wood-Stylist-Turned-Peace-Advocate working for the Dalai Lama Foundation. In other words, he's a pretty open-minded guy.

Yes, he conceded, His Holiness the fourteenth Dalai Lama of Tibet (which Brian thankfully shortened to HHDL) *is* Buddhist, but the purpose of his 1999 book *Ethics for the New Millennium* is to advocate for a moral system based on universal, rather than religious, principles. I was intrigued. In the second chapter (aptly titled "No Magic, No Mystery"), HHDL explains why, even as a religious leader, he doesn't believe religion is essential for living well and is the first religious leader I've heard clarify that "many who reject religion do so out of convictions sincerely held, not merely because they are unconcerned with the deeper questions of human existence."[10]

I thought I might have found what I was looking for: a nice, neat list of universal guidelines written by a wise, studied Nobel laureate, *New York Times* best seller, and an old guy, to boot. But while his chapters on personal ethics—on restraint, virtue, compassion, suffering, and discernment—are as insightful as one expects from such a figure as the Dalai Lama, it's what he writes in the preface that makes me realize I need to approach morality for my children in a radical new way. "Rarely, if ever, is any situation totally black and white," he writes. "The same act will have different shades and degrees of moral value under different circumstances."[11]

As handy as it would be otherwise, understanding morality and developing a moral code—like any existential question religion promises to answer—means understanding *how* to think, not *what* to think. Perhaps the reason the nonreligious have difficulty pinning down what we think about morality, in the way Epstein laments, is that we reject the premise that there *is* a way to pin it down. The relationship between morality and humanity means we must be awfully adept at understanding human nature—all of its variations, complications, glories, and fallacies—to have a strong, developed moral code, and this is not something that happens overnight. This, I find, makes teaching morality more difficult while our children are young but encourages something more sustainable as they grow into autonomous beings.

Eventual autonomy in moral deliberation is one of the most significant things our children take into the world, and allowing for that autonomy is one of the most challenging parts of being a parent. One of our sons in particular can drive Chris and me a bit crazy with all of his arguing and "talking back." When we're feeling optimistic, we call him "our little litigator" and work through the details of our reasoning. When we're too worn down, we just tell him to go to his room.

He's a good kid. He doesn't argue just to argue, like we sometimes claim in frustration. He just thinks more like an adult than other kids. Even as a baby, he looked more like a little old man, steadied and furrowed, compared to his volatile, round twin brother. He's the kind of kid who will probably find a lot of fulfillment in simply being an adult. He reminds me of myself. He questions fairness at every turn, fumes when authority figures assert power without earning his trust and respect, and points out honest fallacies in the logic when he's gotten into trouble.

We treat him, and his strong will, in a way that frustrates parents from previous generations to no end, with our willingness to explain and negotiate. "You have to show him who's boss," they say. "You have to shut down that backtalk." And, in some ways, we are "old-fashioned": our children have daily chores and responsibilities, must know and mind (most) manners, must shake a person's hand and look her in the eye, express gratitude and appreciation. But especially as they get older and are able to reason, I err on the side of my children having too much of a voice than no voice at all. In other words, I'm okay with children talking back when they're exercising their ability to reason and voice autonomy. I don't have the endurance or patience to go every round, so when I do hear myself say, "That's just the way it is" or "Because I said so," I am cringing inside.

My son despises those kinds of answers. When he is crying and raging in his room, he'll say that his least favorite thing about being a child is that the adults have control over his life. They make all the decisions, he says. They might *say* that they want to hear his ideas, but they really just do what they want and the kids have to go along with it.

It's the worst feeling, isn't it? When someone does what they want or tells you what to do or how you must think, disregarding you as a person, and you just have to go along with it? It strips away your dignity, your capability, your sense of worth. How can you treat others well if you do not possess those things?

My son has developed a particular response as a coping mechanism when he feels he's stripped of a voice. Beyond my sight and time with him, he's cultivated a method of standing up, perfectly straight and still, nodding his head with only the slightest touch of zombie in his eyes and hint of robot in his voice, and saying, "OK."

Only after he pulled this number on me a few times did I realize that he *sounds* like he means it, but he doesn't really mean it. To some people, this type of compliance may equal successful parenting, but now that I've realized what he's doing, it makes me even angrier than whatever he's done to bring on the exchange in the first place. It's one of the few times I ever feel like I want to shake my child. I'm not angry with *him*, mind you; I'm angry with myself and the rest of the world that's taught him *you must comply*. That he has to divorce his body from his mind like this, that he'll say one thing while thinking another, reminds me why using my authority as a parent to break his will does nothing for his sense of morality in the long run. Obeying the rules someone else has taught you does not make you a moral person. It makes you compliant. A true sense of morality comes from within, in the places no one else can reach. That moral code will only be as strong and just as the person who is free to shape it.

I'd been having a hard time reconciling my role as an authority figure with my desire to encourage my children's developing autonomy, so I started looking to sources who might help me figure it out. One of the people I came across was pediatrician and parent educator Chris White, who cowrote the book *Mindful Discipline* and founded the organization Essential Parenting, which emphasizes relationship developments between children and parents, with a personal interest in the neurobiology of maturation.

Once I understood the way White reclaims the word *discipline*, I guessed he might be sympathetic to my dilemma balancing my authority with my kids' autonomy. In the first chapter of his book, he's careful to differentiate between the more common understanding of discipline, "punishment," and its verb form, "to disciple" or "to teach." This distinction is crucial, he explains, because "excessive use of fear, guilt, and shame as motivators . . . prevents [your child] from developing the internal *desire* to be respectful and responsible and to do the 'right' thing."[12]

For my children to have an internal desire to do the right thing is what I most hope for as a parent, and this new way of thinking about discipline just might help, so I asked White if I could meet with him and ask a few questions. He lives a two-hour drive north of me in a little pocket of a town known for its affluent-alternative types in a region known for its affluent-alternative types in an entire state known for its affluent-alternative types. So far from a small conservative town in Kansas. I'll admit, I was curious to check it out.

We met at an independent coffee shop, where I put in an experimental order for the coconut-milk latte and vegan-date "brownie" and settled next to a fountain on the patio. Of course, it's not every day that a person agrees to meet a complete stranger for a chat about morality, so I shouldn't have been surprised that White was one of the more curious, thoughtful, and sincere people I've come across in a while. He has two young children of his own and obviously enjoys the overlap of his professional and personal life. White not only clarified for me why my authority as a parent is important for my kids but also pointed to a way to think about morality that is the radical new approach from my own childhood I've been wondering about.

"So, what is it that you're going for?" he asked, after I introduced myself and provided a bumbling definition of what I meant by morality. "As a secular parent, you have to ask yourself, *How do I hope this turns out?* That way, you can fall back on the science. To me, the question is, how do you support the natural ability for your kids to grow high levels of morality? To do the right or good thing, given any situation, that doesn't rely on a rule book."

Whoa. High levels of morality? There are levels? What levels?

"You know, Kohlberg's stages of moral development? Based on Piaget's work?" he asked, a fair question, as I'd told him I'd been thinking about and researching morality for months.

I swirled my head in a sort of tilted nod that said, *That-sounds-familiar-but-I'll-have-to-Google-it-later.*

He gave me a quick summary of Lawrence Kohlberg's theory of moral development—stages of moral reasoning that increase in complexity with proper maturation—with this point of emphasis: as parents, we have to be with our children where they're at, developmentally.

"Because if you move past people and stretch them ways they're not ready to be stretched," he explained, "you tear things, you break things. You don't let the foundation build."

The initial understanding our children have of morality (indeed, the first way *I* understood morality) is that it consists of standards made up by outside authority, and the motivation to do good is to avoid punishment.

"But if you harp on them with punishments and rewards," White explained, "they get stuck. They stay focused there. It's like a muscle. That part of the brain will be used over and over again, and that will be the focus."

When he explained it this way, I understood why I'd been so sure that a comprehensive moral code was something I could find from an outside source and teach; this is, after all, the religious model of morality I'd grown up with. I'd been a little stuck there myself. And it's a completely normal stage of moral development. Kohlberg called it "preconventional morality," and until a child is around nine years old he does look to authority figures for the rules, which is where my role as a figure of authority comes in.

In the same way he does with discipline, White approaches authority as something that can be nurturing and positive. The true value of parents' authority, he explained, is not about being able to boss our kids around (despite what my son might think when he's stuck in his room); it's about assurance. Our authority as parents lets our children know, as White puts it,

"Mom and Dad got this. They know what's going on. They can protect us, guide us, care for us. We can relax and be kids and do kid things."

The instinct some people have to demand authority may come from a good place, an innate understanding that lack of authority in a child's life can cause her to be anxious, compulsive, or controlling. But demanding authority instead of earning it, or insisting that authority figures not be questioned or admit to fallacy, White explains, destroys the attachment a child needs with caretakers to feel connected and integrate her various experiences. White used the term *integration* a lot in our conversation—he described the highest levels of morality as being the highest levels of integration—so I asked him to clarify.

"Morality can't be codified into a set of strict, individual action rules. It's more as a set of principles you'll have to integrate. That's what integrity is: integrating the disparate elements of your life, over time, into a way that works."

I looked up the word *integrity* later, thinking of its usual meanings—honesty, righteousness, virtue—and wondered if being a person of integrity comes from being a person capable of integration. Sure enough, a less popular definition of the word—*whole*—is the one that best describes what it means to have a high level of integration. I'm not raising kids who will be perfect; that's not what morality is about. I want them to have integrity. I want them to be *whole*.

It's possible for us caretakers, as authority figures, to integrate different elements of our reality as models for our kids: acknowledge and even verbalize our mistakes, our growth, while maintaining an overall sense of control for our children. I asked White about my son, explaining that I don't want to shut down qualities that will serve him well in the future but wear me out in the present. His answer, not surprisingly, was as ambiguous as morality itself: "There's no one specific way to deal with each situation," he said.

"There's a range of interactions that kids need to develop whole. There should be times you ask the child, *What do you think? How do you see it?* But in the fly of daily life, sometimes the parent has to decide. If you give a child enough space, sometimes they'll come up with a version of things that's the same as yours, so it's important to have a time when they can bring questions up."

This is when White made reference to "family meetings," the kind of idea that, like baby books, meal planning, and savings for college, is a fine one but still makes my eyes roll (if only on the inside). I don't doubt we could benefit from family meetings, regularly scheduled sit-downs where we raise concerns and work them together. ("Isolate the conversation to one area instead of letting them wear you out in a daily grind," White suggested.) But after trying to fit blocks of time on the calendar for school, work, activities, meals, chores, and *fun!* I feel like I'm piled to the brim with 1980s Tetris pieces that aren't fitting and just keep raining down. I don't see us following through with family meetings that don't happen in the car, when we're already running late.

Of course, maybe this is part of religious practice that we lack: not the morality itself, but rather a structure that encourages moral reflection. That's what White is saying we need with meetings: a consistent structure in place to determine our principles and values as a unit and work out the inevitable conflict that arises in a unit. While a regular, formal sit-down might not be for us, we can take advantage of the ways the nuclear family structure allows us to practice what White describes as high-level integration: balancing concern for the self with concern for the greater good.

There is, after all, a long road to travel between our initial "me-focused" needs and desires (the kind that result in sippy cups flying across a room) and the ultimate, postconventional morality levels reached by the likes of the Dalai Lama, Gandhi, and Martin Luther King Jr., people who develop personal moral principles based on abstract thinking that may or may not fit in with the laws put together by others around them. This road takes us from immediate concern about ourselves into *slightly* widening circles of concern, at least at first—for those closest to us, who take care of us—with even more widening circles of concern as we develop. The hope is that this circle of concern eventually reaches every living being, but it starts at a home base. Thinking of the family as practice for moral reasoning in order to integrate larger circles helps me, as a parent, gain a little perspective in a tense moment, as well as my kids, when they're butting up against one another in sibling conflict.

Whether it's because of siblings, parents, friends, or just the random nature of existence, our children will inevitably face conflict and struggle. But this can also be another opportunity for them (and us) to practice integration. We can never know or understand all the challenges our children will face outside the home, which is all the more reason to use discipline and authority in a loving way to set limits at home, in part for them to practice with difficulty and, additionally, to encourage the quality of resiliency.

White places great value on resiliency, and he's not the only one: our current generation of helicopter moms and drone dads is inspiring titles such as Jessica Lahey's *The Gift of Failure* and Wendy Mogel's *The Blessing of a Skinned Knee*. But even as I'm aware of and agree with the arguments against such overparenting, I still manage to morph a natural desire to protect children from harm into a desire to remove challenges altogether. It doesn't even have to be *my* kid. Not long ago, my husband had to stop me from swooping in to rescue a kid I didn't even know. Once I agreed to step back and watch the scene play out, I was reminded of something White said: "If we don't let kids suffer and build resiliency, they don't know that they're stronger than they feel."

We had taken one of our sons to his first jiu jitsu tournament. Brazilian jiu jitsu, or BJJ, is pretty new to us; just this past year he and my daughter have taken it up. BJJ, from what I can tell as a spectator, is similar to wrestling, only, instead of a tiny spandex bib, it's conducted in (thankfully) different clothes: my kids wear a belted "gi," a uniform consisting of jacket and pants similar to that in other martial arts.

My son was the only person present in his category of size and belt rank, so he was assigned to "spar" with the next group up. His first match was with a girl about his size but with a more experienced rank. It was a good match: they both proceeded with caution, and his possible advantage in strength seemed to balance her advantage in experience. They went around a long time, the occasional toothy grins perhaps undermining their attempts to appear tough, each earning points, until my son ultimately won the match.

I kept an eye on that girl. There aren't nearly as many females as males participating in BJJ—sometimes my daughter is the only female in her class—and this one stood out. She seemed tough—red-faced and serious—but a bit vulnerable. I don't know if it was the thick, double French braids running parallel down her neck or her somewhat quiet way of bowing to her opponent, or if it was just her age, like my son: the achingly poignant twilight of childhood, double digits but hardly teens. Preadolescence, the tension between oblivion and knowing almost palpable.

The next time the girl with the double braids went up to spar, it did not go well for her. Her opponent was one of the quickest, most aggressive boys at the dojo. Before anyone knew what happened, he had her down on the floor in an arm bar, a joint lock submission that hyperextends the elbow and means instant defeat. She was stunned. Her parents were stunned. I was stunned.

I watched her go to her parents, where she began to cry. Any confidence she'd been carrying was gone. I watched her mother and father tend to their daughter with a recognizable struggle of balance: assurance with concern; nurture with restraint. They held her close and looked around. *Was that fair?*

I watched and watched as the minutes passed and the girl seemed to shrink further into herself and away from the comings and goings of the tournament. It bothered me. I pointed her out to my son. Wouldn't he please go tell her she's good at sparring? Wouldn't he give her a high-five or shake her hand? I thought maybe I would go over there and talk to her myself. Maybe I would accidently shove arm-bar-boy on my way. It made me wonder about this tournament, about anything, really, that causes a kid to question her ability. Maybe we should pack up and leave. Let's head to a place where the kids can ride ponies and eat popcorn and never have to struggle ever again.

But then my husband, Chris, offered a practical, illuminating thought: "Isn't it best for her to be challenged here, in a safe environment with plenty of support, instead of somewhere down the road when she's on her own and might not know how to handle it?"

I got the answer when the junior division of the tournament was over and the owner of the dojo announced the standings. When he called their names, the students lined up on their respective third-, second-, and first-place podiums, where they received medals and applause. As they fingered their medals and smiled for pictures, they turned to one another, with high-fives, fist bumps, laughter, and her face—she was beaming—told me that Chris was right.

Learning that we are stronger than we feel is empowering, yes, but there's another valuable quality that emerges when we face hardships, one required for high levels of moral development. As I've thought about morality and its dependence on our shared humanity, I've thought about the ways suffering can deepen empathy. Indeed, that first universal awakening I had at thirteen was triggered by experiencing depths of pain I hadn't known before. In her book on compassionate living, author Pema Chödrön writes, "Only to the degree that we've gotten to know our personal pain, only to the degree that we've related with pain at all, will we be fearless enough, brave enough, and enough of a warrior to be willing to feel the pain of others."[13]

So this desire we have to protect our children: we must be careful to distinguish between when it's necessary and when our holding back might be an opportunity for them to develop resiliency and empathy. We think of empathy as being most crucial in difficult times: when someone is hurt, or sad, or angry. How will our children be able to empathize if they don't experience disappointment, fear, loss, suffering, powerlessness? As parents who seek to encourage moral development, it falls within our obligation *not* to set up our children's lives so that they avoid challenges and struggles but to teach them to successfully navigate and grow from those experiences. If we aren't mindful of detours we open up for our children when an obstacle is in their way, we may look back and see they've traveled roads devoid of other passengers. We may see a child in front of us who has no idea what it feels like to hurt and struggle and strive, with no idea how to empathize, when the time comes, with someone else.

Many qualities I'd already gravitated toward encouraging in my children—empathy, autonomy, intuition, resilience, and reason—have taken on a new effervescence now that I've been able to articulate that they are, in fact, values that will support their moral development. Modeling to our children that moral development is a worthwhile endeavor in the first place is not something caretakers should take for granted. Letting go of the traditional concept that there's an ultimate authority on moral perfection means that secular parents need to put in some extra work, beginning with asking ourselves some tough and fair questions: Why is the way we treat others important? What principles do I believe in that shape my actions? What do I most value in life? Do my actions reflect these values? How do I balance my own needs with the needs of others? When have I made mistakes? How can I do better?

Even then, after considering these questions, we will still find ourselves in moments of anger, frustration, confusion, frailty, or despair with our children and act in ways that don't back up any of our ideas and words. Just as some of the instructions about morality I was given as a child may have been misguided, some I give to my own children will be as well. Thank goodness for integration—our human ability to accommodate all kinds of experiences. I think of the model from my childhood, God as Father, the ultimate authority on moral perfection. He doesn't deliberate. He doesn't negotiate. He doesn't make mistakes. We parents aren't gods, and we don't have to pretend to be. We need to think things through. We need to compromise. We need to mess up and think about how to get it right.

The most hopeful, inspiring thing I've come to believe about morality is that, once we've reflected on our values and principles, moral development is a practice we can have wherever and whoever we are. Family life, right in our homes on a weekday night, is just as good a place for moral development to blossom as any other. Reaching its highest levels doesn't require a pilgrimage to a faraway land or years spent alone in meditative contemplation. It's not about memorizing a list of detailed rules or abstract virtues with the goal of arriving at a great pinnacle. It's not just the grown-ups of the world asking important questions about treating one another well: *Why? How? What if?*

The more I work on articulating and modeling the qualities I hope to see in my children, the more it feels as though we're working toward something together. One of Chris White's questions—*How do I hope this turns out?*—reminds me that we're in it for the long haul, which, in the heat of a moment, can refuel me with a little more grace and patience. My young daughter's tantrum might remind me that she needs someone to show her empathy. My older son's stony silence could be a sign that he feels stripped of his ability to choose. My own urge to run interference whenever any of them face a challenge should be weighed against the possibility that they will emerge from the hardship with more resiliency and compassion. I soften into a parent who isn't rushing us toward some goal but stopping to consider—to pick up and be picked up—along the way.

4

AWE AND WONDER

*Isn't it enough to see that a garden is beautiful without having to
believe that there are fairies at the bottom of it too?*

—Douglas Adams

The only road that takes us from our home in a coastal redwood grove
to the nearest town, twenty minutes away, is a designated scenic state
highway. The locals refer to it as Skyline because its entire length straddles
the ridge of the Santa Cruz Mountains. When the fog rolls in off the coast,
we are literally driving through clouds. On a clear, sunny weekend, it's full
of cyclists, motorcycles, fast fancy cars, and hikers, all there to experience
one of the most beautiful drives in the country. We've learned to time our
errands and activities to avoid the road during peak travel time; like most
Californians, we rarely talk about the weather in relationship to excursions.
Instead, we talk about the traffic.

I don't have to make special plans to get to this particular highway: I'm
simply on it to run for milk or take my son to soccer practice. But even after
a year of making this drive, sometimes on a daily basis, when the cathedral
of redwood trees opens up and I catch the shimmering Pacific Ocean laid
across the horizon like sky on one side and turn my head to take in perfectly
preserved Crystal Springs Reservoir, with skyscrapers of two major world
cities hugging the San Francisco Bay in the distance, I slow the car and think

to myself thoughts that have no words but fall along the lines of . . . *This. Is. Amazing.*

I will still pull over and take pictures or just watch and look. Between the day's changing light, the fog or clouds, and the quality of air, the views on Skyline are always different. Sometimes we are above the fog and I stare at the clouds tucked into the foothills below, hovering over the reservoir like cotton balls, always disoriented by the feeling that I'm on top of them. Sometimes the silver of the ocean is the same color as the sky, and I can't tell where one begins and the other ends. Other times they are so drastically different, one so deep and substantial, the other so light and delicate, that it doesn't seem possible that *blue* could describe both.

Since moving from Kansas to California, I hear all the jokes and stereotypes:

"You're not in Kansas anymore, Dorothy!"

"I bet you didn't have this in your cornfields!" ("Actually," I tell them, "Kansas produces more wheat than corn." *Not that the difference seems to matter to you.*)

"Was it worth the trade of tornadoes for earthquakes?"

But, no, I often say. Anyone can come to California and be amazed and taken in by its beauty. It's obvious and easy. It's a gift, I think, to be from the Midwest, to know its subtle beauty in the hushed whispers of your bones. The amazement doesn't shout out to you in hot and cold; it's more of a warm, slow secret. The endless sunsets, saturating the sky with colors I've never seen anywhere else. The warm summer nights when teenagers learn to point out constellations from a blanket in a field amid the hum of crickets and occasional buzz of mosquitoes. The stillness of the prairie, those fields of gold where possibilities seem endless, perhaps sprinkled with old, wooden windmills, reminding us of a time long passed. I think those of us who had roots planted there, even when we've severed them, feel the whispers like phantom limbs, reminding us that we've known the beauty of a land in a way that's not easily available to everyone.

My children, however, will not have this gift. They are California babies. The twins were freshly six when we moved here, with blotchy, haphazard memories of the Midwest, and my daughter was not yet two. They were all there, back in Kansas, one night when we were locked out of our home next to the Kaw River, when neither of their absent-minded parents had keys to the house. Instead of trying to find a way inside, we were all content to sway on the porch swing together, surrounded by a curtain of fireflies, comfortable on a warm summer night by the gentle breeze carrying our laughter from this plight on the porch with nowhere to go. They were all there, but they don't remember.

What they know now, their day-to-day experience, is a world I could only wonder at as a child by way of television or textbooks: the great redwoods, a major city, the endless sea.

"Look! Look at the ocean!!!" I say, on our drives to town.

"Mom, we live next to the ocean. We see it almost every day."

"Look! Look at the city!!!"

"Mom. That's San Francisco. Duh."

I still try. I recently took them on a hike near our home to a "fairy ring," a circle of young redwoods that grew up around one of the originals, "old growth," that had long ago succumbed to fire or disease or loggers. I told them I had a surprise for them on the hike. When we got there, we tucked into the eerie shelter of the original parent root crown, four of us able to sit comfortably inside the remnants of one of the tallest, oldest trees on earth, with plenty of room to spare, the new growth surrounding us with protection like turrets.

"Isn't this cool?" I breathed, in a hushed tone, trying to add to the atmosphere.

"Mom. We have one just like this behind our house," one of them said.

"Is the surprise that you brought snacks?"

It's no coincidence that we live where we do. Since the first time I laid eyes on the Colorado Rocky Mountains as a teenager on a high school band trip, I've been determined to live in a place that evokes this type of awe on a daily basis. My husband had a similar epiphany in college on a mountain bike trip to the Canyonlands in Utah. The first road atlas Chris and I shared together was quickly worn to pieces after the nights we spent poring over it, pointing out to one another where we'd been, what we'd seen, where we still wanted to go. It has taken years of searching and struggling, four moves and major pinched pennies in the past five years alone, to find this place where we wake up surrounded by what looks like a magical setting from a Harry Potter movie.

I'm a sensitive person, not only in the colloquial sense with regard to other people and their emotions but also in the traditional definition: the word *sensitive* has roots in the Late Middle English word for *sensory*, which has roots in the Latin word *sentire*, "feel." My *senses* are sensitive: to light, sound, smell, taste, texture. My surroundings make a difference to me. Chris complains that he can barely see in our home at night, with the only light offered through dimmers and lamps. (In the days we were dating, I often used candles. "What is this, a séance?" he asked during our first night together.) The children complain that I play *my* favorite songs too loud, *their* favorite songs too soft. (Oh, the dance parties that break loose when we *all* agree on a favorite.) I'm often the one in our house to clean up a toilet, or trash can, the refrigerator, or various fluids left by pets simply because I sniff out the source of foul odor and must make it disappear before the *days* it seems to take everyone else to notice.

I used to be more self-conscious—you might say "sensitive"—about my sensitivity. Ashamed of it, even. In many contexts, it borderlines on insult: *Stop being so sensitive!* But I've realized in other contexts it's voiced near compliment: *Thanks for being so sensitive.* When I realized the opposite of sensitive, *insensitive*, is almost always referred to in the negative, I decided to believe that my sensitivity can serve me well.

I share this peculiar characteristic with my mom. She's a sensitive person, perhaps even more so than me. Like my children are doing now, I grew up with a mother who nosed her way through our home like a hound until she found the source of a smell, who stopped the car and wept when a certain song came on the radio, who fell to her knees in front of the sunset, clasping her hands and crying, *Ohmygod, Ohmygod, Ohmygod. Thank you, God.*

The only real difference in how my mom and I experience awe seems to be the "God" part. One tiny little word at the end of an exclamation. It's a transcendental experience for both of us. We're both stopped by the feeling that we're enveloped in something greater than ourselves; we're both brought to our knees; we both experience gratitude, wonder, amazement. We both think, "Oh, my!"

She just tops exclamations with "God," and I don't.

This seems like it should be a minor difference, but, as a child, I understood awe—and the sense of vitality it provokes—to be only possible through God. Not only was I told this, but it was also my lived experience.

Most of my earliest memories of awe are tied to religion: the sunrise at an Easter service, the sound of music from the choir, the glow of candles in a dark sanctuary.

After I became the Sensitive Atheist and stopped topping my exclamations with thanks to a mastermind creator, it feels as though I cut out an unnecessary middleman, like I experience awe more directly than I used to. It's like I had a God colander before, or a screened filter, that I shook the experience through and was left without some of the bits. Where before there was God between me and what I was experiencing—a compulsion to stop, recognize, and give credit to *Him*—now there is only the inexplicable, the parts of the universe that I may never understand.

I continue to experience it, when I feel the first rhythms of a song fill my body or take in the view of a mountain range on the horizon or smell the syrupy drippings of lily in the peak of its bloom. I'm a transcendence junkie, always looking for the next fix, which would explain why I need to be next to the ocean, among the tallest trees on earth, walking the dog through an alpine rain forest every morning, sunbeams cutting through the moisture and branches, reaching for a place in the atmosphere beyond anything I can see. An insect doesn't cause me to drop to the ground anymore, the way my son recently did when a tiny spider crossed in front of us on the junior high track, so I keep looking for the things that do.

Perhaps this explains why a recent headline in the *Washington Post* religion section caught my eye: "Is It Pretty Outside? Then You're Less Likely to Go to Church." Sara Weissman reports that a Baylor University study found "U.S. counties with nicer weather and prettier natural surroundings see lower rates of religious affiliation."[1]

I wasn't surprised by the headline; it immediately made sense to me. What surprised me was that the authors actually proved, with data, the validity of their initial, simple observation: a map marking the regional variations of natural amenities was "almost a mirror image" of a map showing varying levels of religiosity. The authors can't yet say *why* this is true and have only ruled out the theory that it is related to settlement patterns, but this is the question they want to explore next.

I've got a theory, considering where I live and how much it means to me to be overcome with car-stopping, jaw-dropping moments of awe on a regular basis. I hear the intensity and appreciation of my own experience echoed in the final chapter of *Living the Secular Life*, Phil Zuckerman's exploration of what it means to be openly secular in America. Zuckerman goes as far as to let the inspiration he draws from awe determine the label he's created for himself when those like *atheist*, *agnostic*, or *secular humanist* don't cut it: he's an "aweist," he writes, believing in "aweism."[2]

I appreciate that Zuckerman dedicates an entire chapter to awe in his book on living without religion for a few reasons. First, it's always nice to hear someone correct misperceptions about a group I belong to: of course religion doesn't have a monopoly on the awe experience. But more important, there's something so primal and urgent about experiencing awe, something about it that connects us to the very ephemeral understandings of what it means to be alive, that it seems worth exploring, for the religious and nonreligious alike.

It's almost as though human beings *crave* awe-inspiring experiences and intuitively feel a void when we don't have them. It doesn't seem to be enough that we can find them in the natural world; we create our own sources, too. I often hear people in the Bay Area, a place of staggering natural beauty and loads of cultural experiences, say this about art or beauty or nature: that it's their "church" to surf on Sunday mornings, or hike, or hit a museum in the afternoon, or visit the ballet or symphony on Saturday nights. It's like we heathens are attending the Church of Awe, our collective attendance numbers quite small, but individually off the charts.

All of this makes me wonder, considering the mistaken assumption that awe is reserved for the religious, though more and more parents are identifying as not religious, what *is* it about awe? Why does it matter? And what about our children? As a child, I experienced and appreciated awe through the church; as an adult, I've plunked myself right next to a scenic highway surrounded by nature preserves. But my kids don't have church, and *any* child's regular surroundings are the only point of reference they know. How do my children experience awe? What does it mean for them? Is there a way for me to help them find it?

My kids may take for granted the scenery that blows me away, but I also watch them go through life observing what must seem like a billion tiny miracles. They may not see past the windshield on a rainy day, when I'm pointing to how dark and gray the sea looks, but instead they are staring at the wipers, watching how long a drop of water has to rest before it gets cleared away. They've experienced their share of national parks through the years—Yosemite, Yellowstone, Rocky Mountain—but are most impressed after dark, when the surroundings are covered in blackness and a campfire blazes through the crisp night air, their marshmallows oozing off a sharpened stick into the pit.

They are captivated by slimy, sticky, chemistry-lab gunk.

It's sort of a cultural cliché that children are filled with wonder that inevitably diffuses by the time they become adults, but I suspect this is a bit of misperception. I realize that the wonder we experience seems to be different; my kids aren't as impressed by the Golden Gate Bridge, and I'm not as impressed by the taste of five different sodas mixed together from the fountain at the gas station. But as I look into awe and its effect on our inner lives, I realize it's not as important that children are awed by the same things we are as adults as much as we encourage and respect that they find awe wherever they do and, in fact, learn a bit from their experiences ourselves.

Here is what a person finds out quickly when she tries to understand more about awe: it's one of the most understudied emotions we've got. Almost all of the research available on awe has been done in the last two decades, and one name, Dacher Keltner, a psychology professor at UC Berkeley, comes up repeatedly in the search. Keltner coauthored a paper on awe in 2003 considered to be foundational. He's been involved in countless other studies, authored several books, and is a founding director of the Greater Good Science Center in Berkeley, a group dedicated to using scientific research to help people live meaningful lives.

The way scientists define awe for research is helpful, as both the cause and the effect are contained in the definition. In that 2003 foundation paper, Keltner, along with Jonathan Haidt of New York University, offered a "prototype approach" to awe, with two defining qualities: perceived vastness (something we think to be greater than ourselves) and induced accommodation (the need to expand our current frame of reference to assimilate the experience).[3] For a 2015 experiment on awe with UC Irvine psychology professor Paul Piff, Keltner uses those qualities again in a more succinct definition: awe is "that sense of wonder we feel in the presence of something vast that transcends our understanding of the world."[4]

A growing number of studies on awe since 2003 have contributed to an impressive list of its benefits. According to researchers across the country, with findings published in peer-reviewed psychology journals, experiencing awe can lower stress levels, expand our perception of time, and improve social well-being. As a parent, I'm especially intrigued by findings that awe encourages altruism and empathy, discourages entitlement and narcissism, and boosts creativity and academic performance.

When I realized I lived just across the Bay from Keltner, I decided to send him a message, hoping that we could meet in Berkeley so I could ask some questions. Like anyone passionate about what they do, he was excited to talk about his work and generous with his time. He recommended lunch at his daughter's favorite vegetarian restaurant, so I found myself crossing the Bay Bridge one bright Tuesday morning, a drive I rarely make despite how relatively close it is to my home. As I navigated city traffic between San Francisco and Oakland, across one of the longest-spanning bridges in the country, my senses were overwhelmed by the sound of construction and horns, the heat coming through my windshield, the glare of the sun hitting the water. I snapped off the radio, sat up straight, and gripped the steering wheel; it was both exhilarating and frightening, the novelty and overwhelm ensuring that I paid attention to the present moment, one of the ways awe contributes to a feeling of slowing down time. Just like that, I found myself in awe on my way to understand more about awe.

It was pretty easy to spot Dacher (who insisted I use his first name, which rhymes with "cracker") outside the restaurant. He looked like what you might expect a California-professor-dude to look like, with longish silver-blonde hair, a state-school hoodie, and the relaxed smile of a person who teaches classes on happiness. As soon as we started talking, I realized he approached our discussion with a premise contrary to my own: I've always thought of experiencing awe as a luxury, like the "peak experience" in Maslow's hierarchy of needs, unavailable until our basic needs are met. Keltner agreed that, until he began his research, he had, too. But after studying cultures across the world, ranging from our own in the United States to the indigenous Himba in Namibia, he believes experiencing awe to be *one* of those basic needs. He listed three emotions he refers to as moral sentiments—compassion, gratitude, and awe—and said, "All of the data suggests these are fundamental to human society. These emotions aren't privileges or luxuries, they're foundational."

That we have an innate, fundamental need to experience awe may explain why the *ways* people experience it are diverse and unlimited: what may be a trigger for one person does nothing for another. I assumed being out in nature was the most common trigger of awe because of my own experience, but worldwide, Keltner explained, the data shows *other people* are the number-one trigger.

"It's their magnanimity," Keltner says. "We have data from around the world, twenty-five countries, and the number-one trigger of awe is always the same: someone's profound generosity. Literally, 'that guy over there gave me food, or helped me out, or saved my life.' Which makes sense, when you consider our hunter-gatherer conditions. If you gave me food when my kid was sick, that would be a sacred moment."

I consider this good news for families with the kind of limited resources we had when I was a child, whether they are financial, cultural, or environmental. Examples of the magnanimity in other people are all around us, Keltner points out. He listed some nearby specifics that have inspired awe in him: a drumming circle in Oakland, a volunteer opportunity at San Quentin Prison, a mural in the Mission District, a pickup basketball game, a big family gathering in the park.

Keltner believes awe is an evolutionarily based emotion we've developed to ensure we cooperate within our social collectives. I think of the social way I react when I'm awed, how I want to share it with someone. I long to articulate the flurry it triggers in my inner being, my brain and heart and gut. When I'm with other people, I want them to stop what they're doing and experience it, too. When I'm alone, I still exclaim out loud, as if someone can hear me. When I'm with my dog, I'm like "Lucy! Isn't this incredible?!?"

Awe experiences make us feel we are part of something larger than ourselves. I didn't know to define it this way as a child, but I remember this feeling of transcendence: *I'm part of something bigger than me.* I remember being triggered to think this way around water, whether it was a swimming pool, lake, or river. In high school, my best friend and I spent many afternoons driving to the small lake in town after ordering chocolate fudge brownie sundaes from the local drive-in, sucking on our spoons and staring at the murky water, more brown than blue: *We're part of something bigger than us.*

It's that humility we feel in the midst of something vast that encourages altruism, the practice of selfless concern for the well-being of others. Keltner and Piff confirmed this theory with their 2015 experiment, providing empirical evidence that people who experience awe are more likely to stop and help someone in need. They conclude, "In the great balancing act of our social lives, between the gratification of self-interest and a concern for others, fleeting experiences of awe redefine the self in terms of the collective, and orient our actions toward the needs of those around us."[5]

It seems that awe experiences may be an antidote to the reported influx of narcissism and entitlement in our current cultural landscape. Keltner doesn't necessarily agree that we, as a society, are as awe deprived as some reports claim, but we mustn't underestimate its importance, especially for our children. He explained that developmental psychologists who study awe in children find that the amazement they feel is a way for their knowledge system to determine what is of value in their social groups.

So how can we encourage awe in our children? I think it's important to understand that what we describe as *awe* for adults is often labeled *wonder* for children. It's easy to conflate the two words, which, as nouns, have almost identical definitions, but *wonder*, when used as a verb, means "to be curious or have a desire to understand." This distinction is important, as it implies that the same questions awe inspires children to ask—to wonder about—aren't acceptable for adults. As though we are supposed to *know* the answers by now. But, even if subconsciously, awe and wonder can still evoke something in us to be curious, to ask questions. One of the core elements of awe is that it vibrates with mystery.

As a child, when I asked the questions wonder evoked, they were usually answered in a certain, consistent version of "Because God." Even the question, if I'd dared to ask, "Why God?" probably would have been answered "Because God."

And while "Because God" wasn't a satisfactory answer to my questions, it shut down the line of questioning. It was *like-an-answer-but-not-really-an-answer.* For whatever reason, the adults in my life weren't comfortable with saying "I don't know," and I certainly don't remember anyone saying "What do you think?"

"I don't know" can be a scary thing to admit, even if it's just to ourselves; perhaps we worry that it will be a scary thing for our children to hear. But these are the types of replies—ones that maintain a general sense of mystery—that psychologist, father, and writer Andy Tix encourages parents to give their children in order to nurture awe. In an article for *Psychology Today*, Tix writes, "When answers are given too quickly and easily, awe may be squashed. Awe seems more likely to thrive in an environment of inquisitiveness and questioning."[6]

Personally, I was relieved by this suggestion. Maybe it's just me—I don't know—but I'm not at all embarrassed to say, "I don't know." I really *don't know* the answers to these questions they've asked, the ones prompted by the vastness of the night sky, the stillness of a sanctuary during a funeral, or the pleading eyes of a woman on the corner who's asked us for spare change.

"How did the universe come from nothing?"

"What happens after we die?"

"Why do people suffer?"

My children are asking me the same questions I've been asking myself for at least three decades, and I don't have a sure answer for any of them. I. Don't. Know.

But I understand why we so badly want answers, even if they are as unclear as "Because God," which, though I didn't understand this as a child, seems to be the religious version of saying "I don't know." The thing is, awe is a complicated emotion. As Keltner's original study in 2003 reminds us, "Awe can be both profoundly positive and terrifyingly negative."[7]

I think of a moment in my life that is possibly my most sacred memory, a positive, transcendent moment I'll revisit in my mind again and again. It was also my most intense, primal experience of fear. It took place immediately before the delivery of my third child. I had given birth already, four years prior, to twins; in theory, I knew what to expect. In theory, this third time, giving birth to just one, should have been simpler, easier.

But things were different. During my third delivery I experienced a much, *much* more extreme *transition*, the last, and usually most difficult, stage of labor. Before contractions started, my intellectual self knew about and expected transition. But once it actually hit, I was confused and terrified.

As the contractions I'd been having for the last eight hours or so became more intense and drawn out, the "breaks" between them becoming shorter and shorter, I suddenly panicked. My husband was right next to my face, as calm and sure as ever, telling me I was doing great, not much longer, just take each contraction as it comes.

Something in me snapped, and I grabbed his shirt, gripped it with tight fists, and pulled him so that our noses almost touched.

"How. Many. More." I hissed, my eyes pleading, willing him to have an answer.

"What?" he asked, confused.

"I want to know *exactly* how many more contractions," I rushed on. "I want a number. You keep saying *You're almost there!* but I need to know exactly how many more or I can't do this. I won't do this. I'm not doing it. Give. Me. A. Number."

The other person present, our midwife (who retired not long after this night after overseeing decades of childbirth) interrupted.

"Maria, you're in transition," she said gently. "He's right. It won't be much longer."

Transition! I thought. *I'd forgotten about transition!* Transition, the stage when contractions become rapid and more intense; the stage when you might begin to shake and feel fatigued and more sensitive; the stage when you might become restless, irritable, discouraged, confused.

A gentle wave washed over me. I let go of Chris's shirt. That was the answer I needed. They couldn't tell me exactly how many more. They couldn't give me a number. But they could let me know that, because so many other women throughout history had been through what I was going through, it had a name. It was a stage. *Transition.*

I looked at my midwife, whose name I would soon be screaming at the top of my lungs during each push, which was the only way I could numb the burning pain I felt as my daughter emerged into the world.

"Norla," I whispered with tears in my eyes, ashamed at what I was about to confess. "I'm scared."

"What are you afraid of?" she asked.

"I don't know. I just feel very, very scared."

"It's okay," she said, and then clarified that she didn't mean *It's going to be okay*, because, of this, no one is sure.

"It's okay to be afraid."

The most positive, transcendent moment of awe in my life had been accompanied by an overwhelming, visceral embodiment of fear. It seems experiencing awe is impossible without touching the boundaries of fear. And what more do we want when we are afraid than answers?

Annaka Harris, author of *I Wonder*, a children's book often recommended for secular parents, has some ideas about how to offer these answers. I recognized a familiar reply in the Q&A on the cover when Harris was asked about her motivation for writing the book. She writes, "At the level of our emotional experience, fear and excitement are close cousins."[8]

The book explores mysteries such as gravity, life cycles, and the vastness of the universe, all while encouraging children to ask questions and adults to be honest about their own uncertainty. While the child, Eva, asks the bulk of the questions in the book, her mother asks the first one—an example, Harris explains, of how children don't have to be the only ones asking questions. And Eva's response to her mother's first question, about why the moon seems to follow them on a walk—"I don't know"—is exactly the point. When we don't know, her mother explains, we get to wonder. By writing *I Wonder*, Harris explains, "I wanted to point to an alternative to the fearful reaction to these concepts that is so often modeled in our culture. They can be wonderful mysteries to *enjoy!*"[9]

I thought about this leap she makes, from fearing mystery to enjoying it. It reminds me of something I read in Keltner's first paper about our attempts at accommodating the perceived vastness of the awe experience: when we are unable or unwilling to restructure our way of thinking to assimilate the experience, it can be terrifying. When we are willing and able, it can be enlightening. Do different people innately gravitate toward one over the other? Can we shape our own tendencies through practice? How do we tip from fearing uncertainty to enjoying it?

I asked Keltner about these things when we met and was surprised when he described himself as a person *not* naturally predisposed toward awe: he describes himself as an anxious child, "rigid and tense." He spoke about anxiety in his family history, "crippling anxiety that's the antithesis to awe: closed, obsessive, focused on narrow things."

It was his parents, he says, who, as experimental, counterculture social activists, encouraged him to question convention, withhold judgment, and try new things. He describes himself as being "on the road to unhappiness" when he was younger but, because of his family and cultural context (he grew up in counterculture hotbed Laurel Canyon), kept having awe experiences—through travel, music, and political activism—that "moved the needle" each time to change who he was. Awe, he believes, can contextualize anxiety.

I know the type of crippling anxiety he describes all too well and think of how often an awe experience provides just the perspective I need to calm down. Combine my sensitivity with how cerebral I am, often stuck in my head with thoughts that increase in volume and no dial to turn them back, and it doesn't take much for the world to feel as if it's closing in on me. *Get out!* I have to tell myself, both physically and metaphorically. *Get out of your head and be reminded that you are just a blip in an incredible universe.*

It works for my children, too. When we find ourselves collectively tense and overwhelmed by the give and take required in family life, a change in perspective resets the mood. This humbling connectedness awe evokes may be an answer in itself to how parents can encourage our children to enjoy the wonders of the world without having to provide specific answers: by just letting them know they're not alone in their wondering. I think of the experience during my daughter's birth, how my fear was satiated with a feeling of connectedness: others might not have the exact answer, but I'm not alone. When Eva tells her mother she gets dizzy thinking about how many grains of sand there are in the world, her mother replies, "I'm sure other people feel that way, too."[10]

The more I learn about it, the more I realize that awe is paradoxical: it's an intensely intimate, personal emotion that simultaneously connects us to others, whether we experience it alone on a mountain trail or as one in a crowd, staring up at a skyscraper from a bustling city sidewalk. The key, Keltner insists, is to make awe a priority in your life, figure out what triggers awe in you and your children, and actively pursue it. Schedule time for awe.

Oh, no, I thought. *Another thing for us to fit into our schedule: awe time.* Because I've noticed this about awe: it doesn't strike, it can't blossom, when we're in a hurry. More than I care to admit, I've had to zip down our lovely scenic highway, subconsciously telling myself, *Do not check out the view,* passing cars when the dotted line appears, shaking my head at strangers on the side of the road taking pictures, because WE ARE RUNNING LATE!

But Keltner was not kidding. It's about rethinking what we consider basic necessities and then articulating those values to our children, he said. When I explained to him that sometimes I don't know *what* is triggering awe in my children, like the time I pointed to the ocean through the rain and they were captivated by the windshield wipers, he put my mind at ease.

"They'll have their own specific versions of awe—and it's their job to be different—but what you can give them is an example of reflection. Something that causes them to think, *there is value in this feeling.*"

Recently, the twins shared a birthday and asked to ride roller coasters for the first time to celebrate. It was all they could talk about: that the other kids in their class had ridden roller coasters and they hadn't. Chris and I were happy to take them to the local amusement park, where we decided to ride some coasters ourselves, something I hadn't done since I was probably around my sons' age. I'd forgotten the way it feels when the car inches slowly up the peak of the track, the moments dragging on in suspense, mere seconds transforming into minutes, hours, in the pit of my gut. I suddenly remembered what I used to experience as a child on roller coasters, that feeling of desperation, when I wanted to scream *I WANT TO GET OFF!!!* knowing that no one could hear me and, even if they did, there was nothing anyone could do about it.

It was terrifying, the primal fear flooding my brain and immediately blurring into exhilaration as we rounded the peak and shot down the track. I grasped the bar in front of me so hard my knuckles turned white; I screamed until my instincts told me to nonsensically cover my ears, close my eyes, and be absolutely silent. Pictures from the park's camera placed at this point on the ride shows my son next to me, his toothy smile huge, his hands raised in the air.

"That was awesome!" he exclaimed when we got off. "Can we do it again!?!"

That was *awesome*, I thought, wondering why just moments earlier I believed climbing into the ride's car was the worst decision of my life.

"Yeah. Yeah, let's do it again."

BENEFITS OF AWE

- encourages altruism and empathy by creating a feeling of connectedness with others
- discourages entitlement and narcissism by creating a sense of humility within a larger context
- lowers levels of stress and anxiety by challenging our current perspective
- changes perception of time by bringing us into the present moment
- boosts creativity and academic performance by encouraging curiosity and new ideas

WAYS TO ENCOURAGE AWE AND WONDER IN CHILDREN

- Establish it as a value by commenting on the things that bring you awe.
- Don't be afraid to say, "I don't know," and follow up with "What do you think?"
- Reassure children that they aren't alone in their fear and wondering.
- Encourage children to experiment with their senses: taste, feel, hear, smell, see, explore.
- Make room for flexibility and spontaneity. Awe can strike when we least expect it—the way the sun breaks through the clouds, a new song coming in through the car radio, a flower blooming on the table—and can change the way we experience time.

COMMON AWE TRIGGERS

- Travel: our perceptions are challenged when we are away from routine.
- Nature: the sky, water, trees, plants, animals, insects, vast landscapes.
- Art: photographs, murals, museums, architecture, lighting.
- Music: let the kids choose! It becomes a soundtrack for their lives.
- Science: think dinosaurs, microorganisms, space, life cycles, and chemical reactions.
- Other people: their generosity, kindness, ingenuity. Use rallies, demonstrations, history, and again, travel, even if it's just across town.

5

DEATH

We are healed from suffering only by experiencing it to the full.

—Marcel Proust

I realize many people probably say this about their grandmothers, but mine was the best. When I imagine my version of a heaven, it is a place filled with Jean. She had it all: compassion, intellect, beauty. She had seven children and twenty-two grandchildren, all of whom have their own, unique stories of a special relationship with her. Proving the heart knows no limits, she managed to make every single one of us as children feel totally *known*.

Adept in domesticity and proud of those skills, she baked crazy delicious pecan pies during the holidays, knew how to clean a fish fresh from the hook, and was so skilled in sewing that she made her daughter's wedding dress. But this was only part of her life. When my grandfather died, too young, more than a decade before her, she sold their home and relocated to our university town, enrolled in classes to fulfill her dream of earning a degree, and started learning Spanish. She joined my mom, sister, and me on a trip to Italy when I was a flight attendant and she was in her seventies, jumping right into adventure travel, when we flew standby, had no reservations, carried backpacks, and had to be willing to sleep on a bench one night at a train station when my lack of planning left us with nowhere to go.

(No, I did not make my grandmother sleep on a bench, thanks to a little Italian boy who ran up to us at the train station after dark yelling, *la chiave, la chiave!* He handed us a single key and led us to what might have been the only available room in Vernazza, a small village buzzing with the evening's news of lost Americans.)

This was my grandmother. She was thrilled when she found out I was pregnant with twins; "I always wanted to have twins," she said. She rushed directly from church the Easter morning I'd given birth, skillfully cradled my five-and-a-half-pound newborns, and went home to prepare the hot meals that she delivered to us for weeks. Along with my mom, she took the babies out for walks in the afternoons so I could rest. A picture of the three generations together made it in the local newspaper that first year, when a photographer captured my mother, grandmother, and twin boys enjoying the patio of a local café, snacking on fresh apricot scones in the sun.

When Jean was closing in on eighty, she participated in a triathlon with several of her kids and grandkids, where a race director had mistaken her for a spectator and told her to leave the transition area. She proudly unzipped her jacket, showing him the race number pinned to her shirt, and he quickly apologized for his mistake.

It was shocking, then, shortly after the triathlon, when Jean was diagnosed with esophageal cancer and given six months to live. The twins had just turned two. I witnessed the love, compassion, and generosity she gave to so many people over the course of her life being returned twofold at the end of it. But I also felt like I was a bit on the outside watching, like the person who'd missed the train in Italy a few years back, as my grandmother died. I wonder if I was in denial that her life could actually be threatened. Hadn't we laughed, since I was a child, at how Jean would outlive us all?

It didn't help that, during this time, the clinical depression I'd struggled with since adolescence hit an all-time low. It's no secret that my first pregnancy wasn't planned. Chris and I had been together four months when a pregnancy test confirmed our suspicions and we spent our first anniversary peering into a bassinet that held two sleeping babies. I was absolutely unprepared for motherhood. And having twins didn't help the transition.

Not that it's a contest, but in the range of depressive mood disorders, postpartum depression must be up there as a possibility for "most isolating" in an already notoriously isolating struggle. How can a woman bear to admit the nightmare of burdens chained to her ankles—the fear that she fails as a caretaker, the graphic imaginings of terrible possibilities, the thoughts like truth telling her it would be best for everyone if she didn't exist—when anyone close enough to hear these secrets is preoccupied and enamored with the very creatures connected to her pain? Women in our culture aren't supposed to be depressed or maniacal when they become mothers; they're supposed to be filled with joy and selflessness and grace. They're supposed to be mothers like Jean. Jean had her first child at seventeen. She had four by the time she was twenty-five, my age when I had my first. She had three more after that. I went over these numbers on a daily basis, like I could solve the equation for postpartum bliss.

Looking back on it, with the perspective now of someone who has healed, with no major episodes in years, I understand how badly I needed help. But at the time, I'd been struggling with depression for so long, I believed my lowest points were along the line of "normal" and, further, with a supportive partner and family and resources, that I had no excuse for being so unhappy, so I mumbled things about "postpartum blues" and "hormone adjustments" to my grandmother when she asked how I was doing.

Chris, my sudden husband who was still somewhat a stranger, was the only one who knew the truth. Chris *lived* the truth, helpless to the reality that I had to quit a job I loved because we couldn't afford childcare, that I was determined to breastfeed twins despite the pain and burden it entailed, that I would call him at work while I was home with our children, only to sob and hang up, with nothing I could say. He was the one who dumped breastmilk down the drain when I drank too much; waited at home with our sons on the evenings I left to drive aimlessly around town, sometimes thinking I might not return; and watched as an empty shell of the person he fell in love with struggled through conversation with family and friends.

Around the time Jean was diagnosed with cancer, I gathered up the courage to seek professional help for myself. Even the smallest decisions—*Should I eat? Should I get out of bed? Should I take a shower?*—paralyzed me, so the logistics of how I might get myself somewhere and who I might see felt insurmountable. But thanks to Chris's job we had health insurance, and one evening I drove myself to a walk-in, urgent-care facility, spoke with the doctor on call, and stepped on a path to recovery.

I started seeing a therapist who, after hearing me talk about motherhood, said that I resembled a person who is grieving. I was furious. I almost didn't go back: Who experiences the gain of two children as a *loss*? But I looked up symptoms of grief and identified with most of them: denial, numbness, mechanical functioning, social isolation, misplaced feelings of anger and envy. I seemed to be grieving my old life, the version of myself I wasn't prepared to give up, the one who existed without this new understanding that there is a type of love only quantified by measuring it against a primal grasp of how much there is to lose.

Slowly, after understanding what I was dealing with, admitting to the pain of my experience, dressing the wound where it was raw, I began to heal. I took medication, went to therapy, studied nutrition, exercised faithfully, sought childcare, enrolled in grad school, and finally came clean to others about my struggle. As Jean was dying, I was starting to live again. I never felt so far from her. It was as if I could face one reality, but not both.

At the end of that summer, we went up north for a week, to Chris's family spot at Lake Michigan. Things were looking better for me. I was connecting with my new family, preparing for my first classes in grad school, feeling like I had a fresh start. I assumed we'd check in on Jean when we got back. But the night before we headed home, I got the call from my cousin.

"We made a chain list of people to call and I have your name," she stalled. "I have to tell you . . . Grandma died just a few hours ago. She's gone."

I love to imagine Jean in heaven: not just sitting around but also running the damn place like a cruise director, teaching the angels how to say "please" in Italian and instructing God to take the pies out of the oven at just the right time. I wish I believed she was looking down on me, to know I made it okay, that I became so competent as a mother that I went on to have another child, that she was looking down on the three of them, who will never know her as I did. I go on daily walks now, as she loved to do, and picture her next to me on the trail in the redwoods—actually in front of me a bit while I struggle to catch my breath. She was hard to keep up with.

I think to myself, *Grandma, you would love this if you were here*, and long to hear her cracked honey voice whisper, *I am here and I do.*

But wishing something were true, even with fingers crossed and eyes closed and hearts covered, does not, in fact, make it true. The reality is that no one knows what happens to our consciousness after we die, and the idea of an afterlife seems based on wishful thinking more than actual evidence. My best guess, thus far, is that we return to the state we were in before we were born. This can seem like a bigger bummer than believing in heaven, I know, but, then again, the idea of heaven was never very comforting to me as a child anyway. I was taught that heaven and hell were interdependent, that one can't exist without the other, and instead of taking comfort in the promise of eternal bliss, I worried more about the threat of eternal torture.

It was Jean who took me to the first funeral I remember, when I was around eight years old. Most summers, my sister and I stayed with our grandparents for a week, and Jean took us around everywhere she went. Water aerobics, grocery shopping, coffee with friends. One day she said, "We're going to a funeral," which made it seem normal and helped me understand this is another thing people do sometimes.

I don't remember much about the specifics: who had died, if Jean was close to the person, how much the loss affected her. I do remember feeling very honored that Grandma would bring me along. I wanted to dress in nice clothes and sit among adults on my best behavior to prove I could handle such a serious event. It was a religious service, and I wondered why dying was a sad thing when we were so sure the person was in heaven. Wasn't this life just a test to get to heaven, where we all wanted to go? Shouldn't we be happy that the person had passed the test?

The next memorable funeral I went to was for Jean's husband—my grandfather, Ned, who died when I was fourteen. It was in the same town as the other one—it might have been in the same church—and what I remember most about this one was how close I felt to my family at a time when I felt ostracized at school. All the family—parents, aunts, uncles, siblings, cousins—went out for ice cream after the service, and someone cracked a joke or shared a funny memory and we all started laughing. At first, I was self-conscious: Is it okay to laugh the day of a funeral? But I watched my mother and her siblings hold one another, crying and laughing at the same time, and yes, my grandfather had died, but his death brought us together where the love was so hot it could melt the frozen treat I was holding. I didn't want it to end.

Nine out of ten children experience the death of a family member or friend by the time they complete high school, and my experiences happened to fall in the predictable pattern of losing grandparents before other family members.[1] For this, I feel self-consciously fortunate and undeserving.

My children, too, thus far, have not lost anyone immediately close; the first funeral they will remember was for Chris's grandfather, and the next was a memorial for the father of one of their friends. But however the reality of loss in our lives takes shape, it *is* inevitable and pushes us to think and talk about death, grief, and suffering, perhaps some of the biggest motivators for supernatural possibilities.

As someone who is not religious, I view death very differently than the adults from my own childhood, which means I'm sometimes not sure how to talk to my kids about it. After dropping any consideration of an afterlife, I've come to believe that having one shot at existence is what makes it so extremely precious. The idea that *nothing* happens after we die (or, as always, *I don't know the answer*) is just as valid a theory as any and, perhaps, easier for children to grasp than other mystical promises.

The award-winning children's book *Duck, Death, and the Tulip*, by author and illustrator Wolf Erlbruch, takes an approach to the topic that is both jarring and refreshing to a parent with my background. It reminds me of the classic *Where the Wild Things Are*, by Maurice Sendak, as the protagonist gets to know what he fears in order to grow. In the book, Death is personified, a haunting but gentle character with a softly illustrated skull-head and checked robe.

"For a while now," the book begins, "Duck had a feeling."

Duck is startled when he first noticed Death beside him, who replies, "You finally noticed me."

Death explains that he will be a lifelong companion.

"Are you going to make something happen?" Duck asks.

"No," Death replies. "Life takes care of that."[2]

As Duck accepts and gets to know his strange companion, they become friends. Having Death around encourages Duck to think about purpose and the afterlife. At one point, Duck even warms Death when he gets a chill from their swim. While the point of the book is to offer no clear answers but to think about the questions, I'm reminded of a quote by Austrian poet Rainer Maria Rilke: "Death is our friend precisely because it brings us into absolute and passionate presence with all that is here, that is natural, that is love."[3]

Why some people don't get a chance to experience the natural progression of life before death—those who die young or suddenly or tragically—I don't know. I don't think there is a reason. It isn't fair, and it doesn't make sense, and it's not right. I suppose it's my despair at this injustice that also creates an underlying, regular sense of urgency that I must not take life for granted, an urgency that had left me when I was most depressed. That expression—*live each day like it's your last*—I admit, can be overwhelming, to experience every moment with such intensity, but living my *life* like it's my last, this I can do, with gratitude and amazement that I get a chance in the first place.

I think of this—this chance to appreciate the life I've been given by making sure I'm fully present in it—as a way to honor Jean's memory: my way to reconcile an existence filled with both regret and hope. I was only becoming a person I wanted to be at the end of her life, and I wish she could see how I've changed and grown. But as her granddaughter, I'm listed officially as one of her survivors, and this idea—of being a survivor—is how I approach the reality of loss and suffering.

That we are considered "survivors" when a family member dies catches my attention, because it's often how I describe the type of bond I have with my sons after experiencing postpartum depression. Through the grief I experienced during my transition into motherhood—when hearing the ubiquitous instruction to *Enjoy every moment!* from well-meaning acquaintances crippled me with guilt and sadness—I believe that the twins and I emerged with a relationship that isn't the typical textbook expectation mothers have with their newborns, but rather something different and more stubborn, like scar tissue. We've healed together; we are survivors together. Each experience of loss, each experience of suffering, gives all of us a chance to practice what we are, those of us among the living: survivors.

When I was recovering from the loss of my religious identity and, later, postpartum depression, I found comfort in a model of grief outlined in the 1969 book *On Death and Dying* by Swiss psychiatrist Elisabeth Kübler-Ross. A response to her work with terminally ill patients and her frustration with the lack of training in medical schools on the topic, Kübler-Ross collates five stages of grief: denial, anger, bargaining, depression, and acceptance.[4] The model can be expanded to include any type of personal loss, such as the loss of a relationship, or a loss of identity, or onset of chronic illness. While the model is valuable to some people, Kübler-Ross acknowledged later that her work was sometimes misunderstood, as the stages are neither linear nor predictable. Critics point to a lack of empirical research and evidence for the model, so it's worth noting that new psychological research points to *resiliency* as being the defining factor of grief, which supports our "survivor" label. As Wendy Thomas Russell points out in her book, *Relax, It's Just God*, this understanding of resiliency after loss—that we can give our children confidence that they will be able to overcome suffering—is important because "sometimes, our fear of death comes down to our fear of grief."[5]

Indeed, I consider the first time I realized my fear of grief in the form of a baby bird. When I was a child, my mother (wisely, I've come to realize) refused to give into our pleading for pets because of the extra care they require. I suspect, too, that she was hoping to shield us from the pain of loss that we ended up experiencing anyway, as my three older brothers still managed to sneak animals into our lives, scooping up stray cats and injured reptiles and keeping them in crates and boxes under their beds or on the back porch.

One of these rescues was a young robin that had fallen out of its nest. My brother, the middle one, a big, burly, defensive tackle on the high school football team, found the bird on a sidewalk, constructed a home for it out of cardboard and newspapers, propped up a warmer lamp, and gave it water and food with a dropper. Often we come to love those we nurture through the very act of attending to their needs, which is just what I witnessed as I watched my brother try with everything he had to give this animal a second chance. I overheard my mom warn him that birds this young don't often make it without their mothers, but, at least for a few days, it looked like this one might be an exception.

Alas, the bird died. I found out in the morning, before another day at elementary school, when I saw my brother—in between man and boy—doing something I rarely saw him do: cry. I looked at the bird, a tragic embodiment of hope lost. I poked its limp body, studied its eyes, open but fake, like beads. This is the first time I saw death up close. I did not mourn then, not at home. I seemed to sense that this response was reserved for my brother. I just absorbed, bearing witness to his grief, and made it until lunchtime, when I broke down alone at a table in the cafeteria over a bologna sandwich.

"Why are you crying?"

I don't know anything about the adult on lunch duty who asked me this so long ago, other than she was female, had a sweet, sincere voice, and wore a soft sweater that I felt against my skin when she wrapped her arms around me. I told her about my brother and the bird and she attempted to comfort me, saying those words that, to some, can feel like balm poured over a wound: "That bird is in heaven now."

But I only cried harder, and I knew, I may have even told her: I wasn't crying for bird. I was crying for my brother. Even then, through confusion over the afterlife in my childhood, my lists of who might make it to heaven, and who might not, grief was grounded in the ways death affects the living.

Back then I was, as I am still sometimes now, terrified of the power of grief. When a person believes that death is simply the end of our one conscious go at life, there is really nothing to fear about what happens after we take our last breath. It's being able to manage the grief, pain, and suffering we can't escape *before* we take that last breath that I hope to embrace in the same way I managed to heal from depression—facing the reality of it, dressing the wound where it's raw—and the more I witness my children suffer and grieve, the more I notice that their intuition guides them to approach loss this way all along.

I wondered who I could talk to about different ways children process death, grief, and suffering outside of religion, and I got an idea from something I'd seen during a visit to the nearby UU fellowship. Once a month, the fellowship offers donations to a local nonprofit organization and invites them to speak about their mission. I'd heard several of these presentations, but the one about Kara, a grief-support center in nearby Palo Alto, stood out in my memory. Kara offers children and teens opportunities to connect with peer-support groups consisting of kids the same age who are grieving the death of a close family member or friend. Each summer Kara runs Camp Erin, a sleepaway grief camp for children ages six to eighteen. As a testament to my naiveté and limited experience, I was both surprised that such an organization is needed and relieved that it exists.

Over a year after learning about and donating to Kara, I called their main office and explained that I was writing about death and grief for families who aren't religious. I spoke with Beth Keller, the director for children and family services, and, at first, she seemed hesitant to talk to me.

"We don't want anyone to feel they wouldn't be welcomed here because of religious beliefs," she explained. "It's important that people understand we all process grief in different ways and that it's connection with others who are in the same process that's helpful."

When I clarified that this is exactly what I'm wondering about—a place to turn to outside of church for people who are grieving: What is their approach? Who do they serve? What can we learn from them?—her voice perked up with enthusiasm: "You know who you should *really* talk to, if you can track her down? Donna Schuurman at the Dougy Center in Portland, Oregon. We model ourselves after the Dougy Center, and Donna is known internationally as an expert in childhood bereavement."

At this suggestion, I looked up Donna Schuurman and understood why Keller pointed me to her. Schuurman started out as a volunteer with the Dougy Center (the country's first peer-support center for kids) in 1986, joined the board of directors, and became executive director in 1991, where she served for twenty-five years. In 2015, she transitioned to a position that allows her to work in worldwide advocacy and training. She's the author of *Never the Same*, on grieving the death of a parent, and has provided assistance after such disasters as the Oklahoma City bombing, 9/11, and the Sandy Hook school shooting.

Keller had mentioned that, because of her schedule and travel, Schuurman might be hard to reach, so I was very surprised to be talking to Donna on the phone within twenty-four hours of sending my first message. She, too, was hesitant when I first explained my interest in the center, with a response that sounded a lot like Beth Keller's.

"It's important to us that the Dougy Center is a welcoming place for anyone who is grieving, no matter what their beliefs. Grief looks different for everyone, and it's unpredictable. Kids talk to each another openly about different ideas and they'll ask me, but I tell them it doesn't matter what I think."

Like Keller, when Schuurman understood a bit more about my questions, she opened up and invited me to visit the Dougy Center during a brief window she had between trips to Michigan and Scotland for consultation and training. I booked a flight to Portland while I had her on the phone.

The morning of my visit, the Portland sky was heavy with clouds and the streets were wet. The Dougy Center, located in a residential neighborhood, was easy to spot: I'd seen pictures of it and knew to look for a traditional Craftsman house with white overhanging eaves and a big, welcoming porch. I'd arrived early, wanting to stay dry and not sure where else to go. When I walked through the door, I noticed how cozy, bright, and familiar it was, like walking into a house I'd been in hundreds of times before. If it weren't for the built-in reception desk across from the front door, I would have forgotten that this wasn't actually someone's home. I passed through a large living room filled with several overstuffed couches, a fireplace, and children's table and chairs and peeked into an eat-in kitchen where I heard voices. Two early-shift staffers were having coffee at a long wooden table flanked with benches on each side, the perfect spot for a big, family-style meal. I wouldn't have predicted the overwhelming presence of joy in a children's grief center, but, indeed, joy radiated through every room.

Donna rushed in soon after, worried she'd kept me waiting even though I was uncharacteristically early. Moving and speaking with ease and energy, with a bit of a no-nonsense demeanor, she struck me as someone who is present and grounded in the moment, connected to the person in front of her. When I commented on the beauty of the house, she laughed: "It's the home none of us can afford."

She explained that the original structure was one of several in the neighborhood that had been destroyed by arsonist fire in 2009. After three years of renting elsewhere and dealing with insurance protocol, the board turned the tragedy to their advantage, working closely with architects who were willing to learn from children and families themselves what they wanted in the new space.

The Dougy Center is named for Dougy Turno, whose framed portrait and story is on a wall near the entrance. Dougy was diagnosed with an inoperable brain tumor when he was nine and died at thirteen. In 1981, before his death, Dougy had written a letter to Elisabeth Kübler-Ross, asking her, as Donna paraphrased to me, "Why won't anyone talk to me about the fact that I'm dying?"

Originally from the South, Dougy headed to Portland for treatment, so Kübler-Ross connected him and his family with Beverly Chappell, a registered nurse and pupil of Kübler-Ross's work. At a time when there was almost no understanding of childhood bereavement (or even acknowledgment that children do, in fact, grieve), Chappell observed Dougy's desire to talk openly about dying, fear, and grief. He got other children in the hospital to talk, too, and Chappell realized how the children were able to help one another. In 1982, she founded the Dougy Center.

A good way to understand the center's approach to childhood bereavement is to take a look at the rooms themselves, each located off a circular hallway with a rotund meeting room in the middle. In addition to the children's discussion rooms, divided into four different groups between the ages of three to eighteen, there are also creative play rooms arranged by activity: music, drama, games. After their opening circle, children are free to decide how they want to spend their time, an important way to give them some control during a time when they feel otherwise powerless. As Donna explained some of the idiosyncrasies in the rooms, I began to see a pattern emerge.

In a toy room for the younger kids, stocked with a sand box and organized baskets of dinosaurs, trucks, and blocks, she pointed out the basket containing doll-sized headstones, caskets, and other somber-looking trinkets.

"We started out with Disney and Barbie dolls, but this is what they gravitate to. They line the tombstones in the sand and play funeral."

She showed me an impressively realistic hospital room, with a single bed, retractable privacy curtain, rolling vitals monitor, and a lit screen to read X-rays.

"The kids want to be doctors and nurses, the ones who heal and save. I glimpse in here and see volunteers playing the patient, covered in bandages."

We stopped by the art room, a bright, open space with tables, lamps, and art supplies. Donna drew back a canvas drape in the corner to reveal a room the size of a large closet, covered with colorful streaks of paint, from floor to ceiling.

"This is the paint-splatter room. It was inspired by a boy whose brother had been shot in front of him and he kept talking about the way the blood looked on the wall. He needed to process it, re-create the image over and over, and then one day, he was able to let it go."

Donna had story after story about experiences that brought kids to the center. Depending on the need, the groups sometimes divide even further for kids who have lost someone due to a "typical" death, a traumatic or violent death, or suicide. I noticed that she explained these things in a neutral, nonjudgmental way. She neither built them up as dramatic events nor dismissed the gravity of them. She simply spoke about them as things that happen.

Because of her straightforward demeanor, I soon noticed my reactions to the stories—the boy whose brother had been shot, a mother who died of cancer, a father who jumped off a bridge—widening my eyes, covering my mouth, shaking my head. I was suddenly aware that I was actively trying to distance myself from someone else's experience: thinking that I couldn't handle it, or that these were things that happened to other people. I felt a bit ashamed of this.

I asked Donna about it, this response and others like it: when someone says "I can't imagine" or "I could never be that strong" in the face of grief.

"While people feel they're being helpful, that kind of response can really hurt," Donna explained. "It turns the focus onto the person saying it and away from the person in pain. Now you're looking to them to make you feel better. You don't *need* to imagine it. And no one *wants* to be the one who overcomes tragedy."

When Donna's father died fourteen years ago, she explained, everyone around her said, "I'm sorry."

"What I really wanted to do was talk about him," she said. "I wanted someone to say, 'Tell me what he was like.'"

Kids, too, want to talk about and remember loss. The round hallway is lined with bulletin boards with the words "We Remember" above them, where children bring in pictures of the people who have died. There's a reason that the table in the kitchen is so big: "We have memory potlucks," Donna said. "People bring in dishes that remind them of the person who's died. Maybe it's something they cooked or their favorite food. It's really important to have concrete, tangible ways to remember."

I think about the paint-splatter room, inspired by the image of blood on the wall. Kids are straightforward and *real*; they are literal, visceral thinkers. They want to work through what they're thinking and feeling in ways that may make us grown-ups uncomfortable. But, Donna explained, even though it may be our instinct to want to protect them from suffering, "Kids are saying to their parents, 'Stop trying to fix everything. Stop trying to make me feel better.' They need to feel what they feel."

Younger children, in particular, consider death in concrete, functional ways; until they are around six years old, most think of death as being temporary, reversible. So when a five-year-old sees a dead squirrel on the road and asks, "What happens when we die?" and I get all nervous and fidgety and construct a way to approach souls and spirits, my husband replies, "Our hearts stop pumping blood," and the child nods sagely and moves on to whether we will be stopping for ice cream.

Donna explained that kids want us to be straight with them: "I've never heard a kid say, 'I'm glad I was lied to.'" In fact, it's the euphemisms, platitudes, and figurative language that can confuse and scare children.

"Telling a child that God wanted her mother or baby brother in heaven raises more questions than answers: the child wonders, 'Why does God need him more than me? What if he wants more people in my family? What if he wants me?' The idea of angels is another one that is comforting to some people, but to some it can be terrifying."

My children have begun asking people what happens after we die and experiment with their own theories, usually hybrid versions of things they've heard that change as they turn it over in their minds. I've told them about my own guess, but they don't seem very interested in it beyond being just one of many possibilities. All three of the children have gravitated toward the concept of heaven at one point or another; like many of us, they don't like the idea that the end is the end. With no real threats of hell planted in their minds, they seem to approach the reality of death with more curiosity and less fear than I did as a child.

Their individual takes on death seem largely influenced by their individual takes on life. One of the boys is quite scientific and undeterred; he asks more questions than doctors, veterinarians, and entomologists can keep up with. "The Cycle of Life" is his summary for understanding most existential, subjective subjects, from sex to illness to purpose. He answers "What happens when we die?" in a concrete way—we become decayed matter that nourishes the plants that feed the bugs and so on.

His twin brother, a more abstract, squirmy thinker, ponders different types of questions: *Does it make sense that we have souls? If so, can they "go" somewhere? How can they recognize one another without bodies?* He processes grief more quietly than the others, retreating into his mind without a sound, sometimes emerging with voice to his thoughts and questions, sometimes not.

The variety of ways my children think and talk about death reinforce the initial message I heard from both Kara and the Dougy Center: that everyone grieves differently. After seeing the space and meeting the staff, it was clear that absolute openness and acceptance is crucial. Children need a place without judgment and taboos. Schuurman is particularly proud that the Dougy Center is able to run an open-ended program with no time limit for participants. The average time people stay in the groups, which regularly meet every other week, is fifteen months.

"This allows them to get through the first year and the dates that are hard to face: holidays, birthdays, vacations."

This is a place people don't want to leave. Almost every staff member Donna introduced me to had originally come to the center as a participant, either for their children or as a child themselves. I heard similar statements: "This was the one place I didn't feel alone," one staffer told me.

"This is the only place I could be myself," said another.

"Really, that's what it's all about," Donna told me. "The power of people getting together to tell their stories."

It seems, as a culture, we're not so sure about addressing death and suffering directly. It's something that happens behind closed doors. After my day inside the Dougy Center, I stepped back out on to the sidewalk thinking of how compartmentalized American life is. Had I realized how many people are grieving all around me? But can't we also open ourselves up to the fact that life presents regular practice for grief?

After my sons' birth and postpartum depression coincided with my grandmother's death, I can't help but consider birth and death as two sides of a wondrous, maniacal, extraordinary coin. The experience of being so wrapped up in a child's life is a practice in delighting in the person he becomes while grieving the person he leaves behind. Children change so rapidly I'm often overcome with a sudden burst of something like grief at losing a person I knew, even when that same person is still, technically, right in front of me.

I had asked Donna how working at a children's grief center has most affected her.

"It's heightened my awareness of what matters. It's increased my ability to detect bullshit."

She can't write it in a mission statement, but this is what I learned from Donna and what she and the others learned from Dougy: kids can detect bullshit from a mile away. They just want us to be honest, even if that means admitting that we don't know, that we are afraid, that we are sad and confused and angry, too.

The mysteries around death are such wild, ineffable, unknowable things, it makes sense that we're drawn to concrete, human ways to express what can't be dealt with rationally. I see an example of this type of expression on almost a daily basis in our part of the country in the form of bizarre memorials I'd never seen before moving here: ghost bikes.

Ghost bikes are old bicycles that have been painted stark white, from tires to handlebars, and placed at a site along the road where a cyclist has been killed. They are roadside memorials, not unlike the crosses and arches of Mexico and the Southwest, *descansos* (which translates to "resting place"), often adorned with flowers and wreaths and candles.

Ghost bikes get my attention, not only because they're so large and striking but also because I'm a cyclist married to a cyclist, the two of us having met working at a bicycle shop, so the message hits very close to home. We live in and around communities where there are almost as many cyclists as there are powerful, luxury cars, and even with some of the most progressive road-sharing laws in the country, the two collide on a tragically regular basis.

Ghost bikes aren't the only memorials we see in the area: there are those constructed along the particular scenic mountain road on which we live, honoring drivers and motorcyclists who, too frequently, lose their lives during recreational drives. Currently, there's another just down the coast along Highway 1, in front of a particular wave break called "Surfer's Beach," constructed of a teak cross, beads, and hibiscus flowers.

I've heard people describe these roadside memorials as depressing and morbid; an organized group of activists is pushing for laws against them, claiming they are unconstitutional, using public land for what should be a private act. To them, they are a distraction, somehow different from the millions of other roadside distractions along our highways.

The memorials move me. I choose to let them speak. When I see one, I'm at once humbled and reverent, will take a moment to honor the life of a stranger who was so obviously loved and will be missed by others. What did Donna say? *It heightens my awareness of what matters.* As I attempt to make the subject of death accessible to my children, I'll point out the *descansos* myself, if the kids don't spot them on their own. *Why not?* I think, considering we're bombarded with messages throughout the day that only seem trite—*The new iPhone is out!*—when held against these public reminders: loss is everywhere, it's inevitable, and it hurts.

My children have recently experienced a meaningful loss, one that reminds me of the things I'm still learning: that to suffer is a practice; that sometimes the most devastating circumstances to a child are those that might be dismissed by an adult; that we search for and need concrete reminders to express what we can't with words.

Now that we own our own home and live in a rural area, we've acquired a number of animals. First it was a cat. Then a dog. Then we got chickens.

"These are not pets," Chris tried to tell us. "These are egg producers."

But I challenge any former city slicker to bring home a box of baby chicks and *not* name every single one of them. The kids picked them out themselves, held them, fed them, spread old sheets across the living room floor and built mini chicken houses out of blocks for them. In the same way that happens for any caretaker, the more you work to keep something alive, the more of your own life you give. As the chickens grew and moved from their brooder to the outside coop, the kids brought them scraps of lettuce and "party mix," a combination of crumble, corn, and dried mealworms.

After a few months, we noticed that one began looking quite different from the others. It was black, with the exception of a little white poof of feathers on its head that just kept getting bigger and poofier as its body got skinnier and longer. We looked into it and realized we'd accidentally purchased a white-crested black Polish bantam. I didn't know what the hell that was, either, but basically it's a "show bird." Smaller than a regular chicken and not an efficient layer, they're just fun to look at and not particularly productive.

Chris and I were going to return this crazy chicken to the feed store and get a proper laying chicken, but the kids had already named her Mop Top, and she was one of their favorites. So we kept her. But because she was a bantam, a smaller breed of chicken, Mop Top was the only one able to fit through the bars that separate the chicken run from the dog run, and chickens are a lot of things, but intelligent is not one of them. One afternoon, this is just what she did.

The kids had been at school that day and I had been out. In the moments before picking them up, I had been listening to NPR, the reports coming in of yet another tragic event unfolding on a global scale. As the kids got in the car, I changed the station. I felt self-conscious about this. I always do when

I shield them from difficult things in the media: news, movies, sometimes even commercials. I read and hear about my peers talking with their own children about national or global tragedies and feel self-conscious that I shelter mine, that the horrors of the world might someday hit them as a big surprise.

I'll be the first to admit that my methods seem paradoxical. I don't tell them about mass shootings or child refugees, or even let them watch the latest superhero movie, but I'll point out roadside memorials. I will talk to them about death. I will help them bury their pets. I guess I'm focusing on first letting them practice grief with the immediate losses in their lives: I was honored to bring them to the one funeral we attended last year, that of Chris's grandfather, where they witnessed and experienced grief with and among some of our closest family. But relative to so many other children in this world, mine live an innocently oblivious existence, attending a small school in a rural community with a tight network of adults caring for them.

The very afternoon that I switched the station on the radio and was questioning what they can handle and what they can't in terms of suffering, they ran to check on their animals at home and found the ripped-open, lifeless body of their beloved chicken next to the playful, wiggly body of their beloved puppy. And I witnessed uninhibited, primal, wrenching reactions to loss that paralleled any other.

They screamed. They wailed. They sobbed. They got angry and smashed sticks against trees, cursed the puppy, ran in and out of their bedrooms, collapsed on the floor, refused to eat.

One of my sons, the little scientist, took it hardest. He calls himself "The Animal Whisperer"; he has an intuition with all of them that I can only marvel at. Before we even realized what a strange bird we had, he had claimed Mop Top as his own. Months after this nightmare of an afternoon unfolded, he still refers to her on almost a daily basis. And at night, the times he cries himself to sleep with her memory on his mind, he reaches over to touch the four smooth, black, beautiful feathers he gathered and saved and taped on the shelf next to his bed.

6

MEANING
AND PURPOSE

Tell me, what is it you plan to do with your one wild and precious life?

—Mary Oliver

One morning in June, the kids fresh out of school for summer, I eased out of bed and immediately collapsed onto the floor in pain, doubled over and breathless. I had been living with a disc injury in my lower back for almost a year and had tried almost every nonsurgical treatment possible, with little relief. After months of masking my worsening condition with ibuprofen, enough was enough. My spine could no longer support me. Less than a year earlier, I was backpacking with my kids, climbing the toughest hills on my bike, and perfecting my push-up, and now I couldn't even crawl to the bathroom. I cried out for Chris, who was in the kitchen, as he had been every morning for much of the year, on his own to keep things running while I tried to get through the days. That morning he found me on the floor, carried me to the bathroom, and held me over the toilet, no hesitation. It was one of the more humiliating moments of my life, the words "in sickness and in health" never having such meaning as they did when he supported my weight while I peed.

What were we going to do for the summer? I didn't know how long it would be until I could get off the floor, let alone walk again, and we had three kids at home all day, every day. We couldn't afford to outsource anything.

We had no family nearby, and while friends and neighbors offered to help, we knew they were like us, hustling to keep things running even in the best of circumstances, without a lot of bandwidth to take on new challenges. Chris managed to take a week off work but couldn't miss more than that. The domestic chores I've come to ambivalently embrace over the years—cleaning, cooking, laundry, scheduling, schlepping—fell by the wayside. I knew the work I did at home was of value, but I didn't realize *how much* value until I couldn't do it.

I worried about the kids. Their summer did not look promising. We live in an isolated rural area, and I couldn't leave my room, let alone take them around to swimming pools or barbecues, baseball games or camps, or the number of other activities their friends would write about their first day back at school for "My Summer Vacation." What would they do with their time? How would they have any fun? How would they survive twenty-four hours a day together without losing it? This anxiety was a complete flip of perspective from the one I'd had during the school year, when I worried that they didn't have *enough* responsibilities. Especially in the boys' last year of elementary school, Chris and I had found ourselves repeating variations of the "when I was your age" speech.

"When I was your age, I was babysitting," I told them.

"When I was your age, I was cleaning the entire kitchen by myself," Chris told them.

"When we were your age, we walked to and from school uphill both ways," we told them.

During the school year, we'd given them basic chores and checklists and told them to suffer the consequences from forgetfulness, things we hoped would cultivate responsibility, but it all rang pretty hollow. Nothing seemed to stick. They still complained, argued over fairness, half-assed their jobs, and ran out the door without their lunches and homework, which I usually ended up delivering to the school like a sucker. After yet another round of nagging and lecturing, I would compare their childhoods to my own and silently wonder when letting a kid be carefree and credulous morphed into letting a kid be spoiled and entitled.

My collapse in June quickly put an end to all that. Our children were going to be put to work. We had no other choice. We were lucky, really, that this injury happened when the older ones were old enough to learn to cook and do laundry, clean the dishes and vacuum, and care for their little sister, because this is just what they did. Every day, they woke up and made breakfast, went to work on a list of chores, took a break for some play and screen time, prepared lunch for themselves, and then did more housework in the afternoon, all while checking in on me. Welcome to summer vacation.

As we approached July, I started a new treatment for my injury that began to provide relief, albeit slowly. After a few sessions, the pain receded just enough for my mind to consider how useless I'd become. Since my first babysitting job, I'd worked at least part-time jobs—sometimes up to three at a time—until having children, and even then, when I didn't work out-side the home, I worked hard inside. I was used to diligence, productivity, self-sufficiency, "earning my keep" in the world. I was used to feeling like I contributed to a greater good.

Now I spent weeks in bed—any position other than laying horizontal put too much pressure on my spine—maybe with a venture to the sofa on a good day. At first, I tried to accept my situation. What parent hasn't dreamed about staying in bed all day while everyone else does the work? I was in too much pain to concentrate on much more beyond what the mind-numbing sides of TV, magazines, and the Internet provided. But day after day of mindless activity and limited mobility, with no guarantee of an end . . . it got to me. Never before had I realized how strong and innate the urge inside me was to feel useful. *Not only am I doing nothing*, I thought, *but I'm also creating more work for everyone else.* My mind, as if to compensate for a lack of physical activity, worked overtime and went to dark places. I've suffered through depression several times before and had been warned it often accompanied chronic pain. I immediately recognized the old hissing: *You're worthless. You contribute nothing. It would be easier for everyone if you didn't exist.*

These same old thoughts I'd learned to recognize and dismiss when I was physically healthy grew more relentless: *No, really. This time, you re-ally contribute nothing. You're worthless. It would be easier for everyone if you didn't exist.* I listened to the children's movements outside my bedroom walls, helpless to do anything when I heard a glass break, or water run too long, or the dog whine to be let out.

On top of their new responsibilities, the kids witnessed my suffering to an extent that had to be alarming. The nerve pain I had from my injury came in waves, and they began to predict as well as I could when one was coming on. They would check on me and know, when my breathing was shallow and panicked, when my eyes glazed over, when I began to whimper, that they should call their dad and leave the room if they didn't want to hear their mother moan and watch her weep.

This is too much for them, I thought. *A month ago they could barely handle clearing the table after dinner and finding their shoes in the morning. How are they going to do this all summer? When are they going to snap?*

But one of those mornings, right around Independence Day, after Chris left for work, my son came into my room with major bed head, a big smile, and a bowl of cut fruit.

"Would you like some peaches?" he asked, presenting his offering with a sly grin, like some sort of deranged butler holding back a royal secret.

"Um . . . sure," I said. The peaches were at the peak of their ripeness, gold and gleaming. "But what's going on?"

He burst with excitement and pride, just buzzing with a positivity that countered my own state. "I was cutting this peach for you and realized all of the things I can do on my own now!"

He told me how he handled the peaches just as he'd seen me do it, choosing only the softest, juiciest ones, and prepared them as part of breakfast for himself and his siblings. He'd fried some eggs, the way his dad had taught him, lighting the gas stove and turning the flame down just so to heat the oil in the skillet. He'd cleared the table after he ate, and he also loaded and ran the dishwasher. He'd negotiated with his brother to decide who would walk the dog and who would feed the chickens and set his sister up with a show on TV so he could start a load of laundry. And he'd done these things not only without complaint, without feeling sorry for himself, but also with a fresh spark: an internal drive powered by a sense of contribution and accomplishment. His siblings were in on it, too. Of all the sounds and noises I heard them make outside my bedroom walls, I realized, bickering and arguments were not among them.

While I had been stuck in my own head, feeling worthless and insignificant and wondering whether I was responsible for robbing my kids of innocent, carefree summer days, they were finding a new meaning and purpose behind those days, growing, developing, and maturing in ways I had been previously trying to expedite by nagging and giving lectures. They were living their own "when I was your age" stories they could tell in the future: "When I was your age, my mom hurt her back and couldn't get out of bed, and I had to make my meals and take care of my sister and walk the dog, uphill both ways."

By the time they went back to school in August, I was on the mend. I could walk and drive again and generally participate more in life. I was *thrilled* to return to the drudgery of domesticity. This is when I realized there seemed to be an inverse correlation between my capability and the kids' industriousness. The more I was able to do, the more often I had to remind them to pitch in. The arguments picked up again between them over whose turn it was to unload the dishwasher. The first day of school I got a call from the office: "Your son says he left his lunch at home."

Still, the summer had given us a new standard to measure our days against. We had all gotten a glimpse of how they rose to a challenge and thrived by doing so. We had seen them motivated and focused and proud. What a paradoxical experience it was, for me to despair over being so useless as my children reveled in being so useful. I couldn't get my son's big grin over the cut peaches out of my mind. It got me thinking more about what seems like a natural desire, for kids and adults alike, to feel as though we contribute something to the world around us—to experience angst when we don't and satisfaction when we do. We want to believe there is significance in how we spend our time, understand reasons for the way our lives unfold, imagine the legacies we might leave behind.

The questions around life's meaning and purpose are very different for me now than when I was religious. When I was a kid, the reason for my existence was explained to me long before I even thought to wonder about it on my own, and I suspect my despair over my deconversion would have been less intense had this not been true. The one-word explanation: God. A divine being had consciously created me, and everything around me, for a purpose. The specifics of what this meant for me, personally, were never really clear, but that wasn't so much the point as *there is a plan*. Anything that matters matters because of God, and he created us, above all, to worship him. That was my ultimate purpose in life, one I embraced readily. It felt really good. It's a comforting thing, to trust that someone with infinite wisdom is in charge and has everything under control. (As soon as doubt and skepticism crept in, though. . . . a supreme deity imagined me into existence to worship him? Who *does* that?)

By high school, however, I started doing what teenagers do well: I began asking, "What's the point?" It probably commenced when I was told to memorize the periodic table of elements, but I soon applied the question to life around me, the assumed trajectory of school, work, retirement, and death, with marriage, some babies, and a few vacations sprinkled in. I was aware that my stage in life as a teenager made up the material for songs on the radio by John Mellencamp and Bruce Springsteen, and I was gaining an understanding that once we've spent a moment in time, it's gone for good. Shouldn't we give some thought to these moments like our lives literally depend on it?

I noticed that, regardless of whether people around me believed in a cosmic meaning, they seemed to all be doing the same things. But who decided that this makes up a life? How might it be different if we'd been born in another time or place? Why do people do what we do? What if there is a better way? The older we get, I realized, the more autonomy we gain over how we spend our days, and I wanted to be sure that I was using those days wisely. I wondered how much other people consciously thought about all of our choices—whether they recognized them *as* choices—as we pass through fleeting moments that accumulate to make up a lifetime.

Not everyone was into entertaining these questions, but I found a few like-minded friends who would join me down by the lake with ice cream from the drive-in or for a cruise on country roads with cheap strawberry wine, where we drank from the bottle and wondered why more people didn't ask, "What's the point?" During this time, I still wanted to believe that I was created with some purpose in mind, one that was bestowed from the cosmos, but it was clear to me by then that I would need to take a more active part than I previously realized in understanding what that purpose was.

I noticed that whatever activities my peers and I were involved in— sports, clubs, drama, band, student government, smoking pot—all boiled down to being interesting ways to pass the time. The believers just added that we were doing it "for God" ("I play the flute/score touchdowns/orga-nize prom *for God*"), which, to me, didn't feel like a real purpose as much as an afterthought; instead of God *giving* us a purpose, we came up with our own and gave him some credit so that we could keep doing what we were going to do anyway. Even the potheads were like "Smoking pot brings me closer to God."

During those times of angsty teenage philosophizing, I was struck by two ideas that were very clear to me, two truths that I began to measure my questions about meaning against: (1) an intrinsic awareness that my existence is of value beyond measure, and (2) an intrinsic awareness that this is true for every other person in the world.

(Where did these ideas come from? To this day, I'm not really sure. My family and church community certainly encouraged and reinforced my feelings of worth. And perhaps it's also the way transcendental moments accrue to bring us in touch with a shared humanity: the way sunlight feels on bare skin, the taste of a tomato picked from a backyard garden, the smiling eyes on a familiar face in a room full of strangers. The most essential, mundane moments can be transcendental, even—*especially*—to a child. I'd experienced enough of them to know that life is indescribably special and that I'd done nothing to be more deserving of it than anyone else.)

Regardless, these two ideas, when considered against the immense and indiscriminate suffering I observed, whether it was a news report on a war-torn country somewhere far away or the local family who lost a child in an accident, began to dismantle any belief I had in an ultimate, eternal meaning of life or reason for why things happen. In my mind, if I wanted to be a beneficiary of the hopeful idea that I'm part of a divine plan, then I must carry the burden of knowing that same plan includes a tormented or all-too-brief existence for others that is beyond any justification, divine or otherwise. The thing that made the most sense is that it didn't make any sense. Thinking about meaning leads some people to God; for me, the opposite was true. I wanted out of the plan.

There was a problem, though: I had been taught that God was the source of that awareness I had of the value in existence; in fact, he *was* the awareness. If I were to consciously embrace what I suspected—that I was not created for a prescribed purpose, that there is no divine meaning of life—would my awareness of life's value shrivel up like a raisin? Would it disappear? Would I no longer desire to live a meaningful life?

It would take several years to answer these questions, but, as it turned out, no. My existence still feels as precious to me as ever. Even through immense bouts with clinical depression, the knowledge that I only have this one, random chance to experience life to the fullest kept me going. Although I'd been taught that, without belief in divine purpose, the nonreligious lack hope, the opposite has been true for me. A simple acceptance that life unfolds the way it does for no eternal reason gives me a sense of peace I'd never had as a believer.

A particular parable I heard years ago provided my first secular perspective about weathering the ups and downs of life after leaving religion. It's a simple message that inspires me to let go of a grasping, desperate insistence that everything must work out in a way that us humans see fit. But it's ancient enough in origin to have several titles and be attributed to different schools of thought, so I was surprised when I opened a children's book by Jon Muth, *Zen Shorts*, and found a version of "The Farmer's Luck" written for kids, as told by Stillwater, the panda.[1]

The parable opens by telling the story of a farmer whose only horse runs away. His neighbors, believing he'll need consolation, react to the news with variations of "What a bummer!" depending on their worldview: *What bad luck! What a curse! How awful!* They're confused, though, when the farmer is steady and calm and replies with his own variation of "It is what it is." *Maybe. We'll see. Who can say?*

Soon, the horse that ran away comes back with an entourage of mustangs: healthy but wild horses. This time, the farmer's neighbors believe he'll want to celebrate: *What good luck! What a blessing! How awesome!* Again, the farmer is steady and calm and repeats what he said before: "It is what it is."

The neighbors don't get it. *What's with this guy?* But then, when the farmer's son tries to tame one of the wild horses to use on the farm, he is thrown off and breaks his leg. At this point, you may know what the neighbors will say: "What a bummer!" And the farmer, again, shrugs his shoulders and calmly replies, "It is what it is."

Sure enough, the farmer's luck doesn't seem so bad, after all, when the military comes to the village to draft soldiers for a war. Because of his broken leg, his son is spared and remains at home when the other young men are taken away. Here come the neighbors, with their talk of blessings and luck, and the farmer remains as steady as the day his only horse ran away.

By this point, even young children understand the message: time marches on and events unfold. This fact of life is inevitable. Outside of how they are interpreted by the people making sense of them, these events are neutral.

What we think is bad can also be good. What we think is good can also be bad. What we think is all about us has nothing to do with us. What we think has nothing to do with us can affect us very much. With the perspective of time, it all comes out in the wash.

What is *not* inevitable about these events is our interpretations of and reactions to them. Instead of riding the waves of highs and lows, celebrating our joys without connecting them to our sorrows, we're reminded that each of us are only *one tiny part* existing in a world that's been unfolding long before us and will continue to do so long after we're gone. We simply work with the time we have.

When it comes to questions of a prescribed, divine, or eternal *meaning of life*—a grand reason why we exist and why life unfolds the way it does— I'm content to accept that there is none. It's the ultimate lesson in humility. When nonbelievers are asked what gives life meaning, we will typically say that meaning isn't bestowed upon us; we make our own. Besides the God part, the specifics are the same for everyone: we find meaning in connections with family, friends, and community; attachments with our children and pets; a satisfying job or hobby; contributions to a need or cause; beauty in nature, art, and music. We don't need a guarantee that our individual lives fit into an eternal plan when we can see the real-time effect we have in and on our immediate environment and the people we share it with.

From the moment I began to think more deeply about purpose and meaning, whether eternal or not, the ultimate, ongoing concern I have is with how it informs the way I spend my time. Keeping in mind those two truths I've considered since adolescence—that we're all equally living a life of value beyond measure—the reality is that we are all *also* born into wildly different circumstances and environments. People face all kinds of variations from the start, whether they are huge and obvious or small and subtle; whether we label them as advantages or disadvantages—potential for damage, potential for growth. The one equalizer for everyone is that we each have twenty-four hours in a day. What one person considers a meaningful way to spend her time will inevitably be considered wasteful by another, so the best I can hope for is peace of mind with how I spend the hours that add up to make a life. Author Annie Dillard captures this sense of urgency I have about time (and explains why I was so devastated during the weeks I spent in bed) in her book *The Writing Life*: "How we spend our days is, of course, how we spend our lives. What we do with this hour, and that one, is what we are doing."[2]

I notice and am inspired by how even the youngest children experience a sense of determination, fulfillment, and satisfaction when they believe in a purpose behind their actions, spending an entire afternoon lining toy cars end to end, collecting little treasures to hide in pockets of their home, tirelessly digging holes in the yard outside with spoons from the kitchen. Who would tell them these are meaningless endeavors? How do we hang on to that profound sense of purpose as we grow in a complicated world?

We're unique, us humans, in the way we are aware of and question our own existence: why we're here, what our purpose is, the meaning of it all. Ever since those adolescent days down by the lake, I've found meaning in thinking about meaning. I don't have the kind of prescriptive answers for my kids that I was given as a child, but I do find value in the questions. And like questions on morality and mortality, it's going to take some thoughtfulness and intention on my part to lay a foundation for my own children that won't be set by the church.

As I look into what seems like a universal desire to explore questions of meaning and purpose, I find that the science of purpose and meaning, like scientific studies in other topics historically explained by religion in this new, secular age, is in its infancy, but blossoming. Emerging research in psychology, cognitive neuroscience, and other medical disciplines brings us new ways to understand the practical and biological impact of considering timeless philosophical questions. Not only do people who feel that their lives are meaningful live longer, but they also have a strong sense of purpose in life that has been shown to support the central nervous system, reducing the risk of Alzheimer's disease, stroke, cardiovascular problems, and inflammation.[3]

Because I was taught to understand meaning in the context of religion, I wondered what a meaningful life looks like for someone who doesn't believe it's prescribed or divine. Does it count for people like me, who've determined it's up to us to make our own meaning? I found a simple, yet extraordinary, clarification offered by Michael Steger, who is known in the field of psychology for his "Meaning in Life" questionnaire, in the *Time* article "How to Help Your Kids Find a Purpose."

A simple little preposition adjustment can change everything: Steger explains that "there's a difference between meaning *of* life and meaning *in* life," and people like him are interested in studying the latter. Even for people who aren't concerned with the more abstract meaning *of* life, the idea that your personal life is meaningful is "tightly tied to being happier, more positive, more confident, more caring, more helpful, more resilient, and more satisfied in your life, relationships, and work."[4]

Something that struck me about Michael Steger's resume is that, in 2012, he established the Laboratory for Meaning and Quality of Life at Colorado State University, where he and his team conduct surveys and experiments to explore and measure meaning. I was curious to know more about a guy who has the chutzpah to create such a lab and how, exactly, a laboratory for meaning works, so I sent Steger a message and asked if I could meet him on campus. Selfishly, I looked forward to returning to Colorado, the first place I'd visited outside the Midwestern plains when I was fourteen, for a school trip. I remember when I spotted the Rocky Mountains emerge on the horizon like turrets on the earth's crown. I jumped off the school bus at the end of that week, faced my parents, and declared to their amusement, "There's so much out there to see!"

After Steger accepted my self-invitation, I made my way to the CSU campus in Fort Collins, a bustling college town in the foothills north of Denver, at the base of the northern Front Range, on a brisk October day. It was certainly an obvious setting in which to ponder significance. The town itself transmitted a determined sense of purpose—a knowing for why it was there, the way university towns often do. The trees were magnificent shades of amber, sienna, and chartreuse, foliage from a crayon box, and students hustled through campus in boots, jackets, and scarves on lunch break, clearly with places they needed to be. I was reminded, as I always am when I travel, of how much is going on beyond any one person's experience.

I found Steger in his office in the Behavioral Sciences building and realized I'd probably let my imagination get the best of me. I suppose I was expecting to meet a weathered man in a dim, cavelike room, hunched over ancient scrolls, wearing a robe and maybe training young Jedis with gestures of his hand. Instead, I found a tall, sprightly guy in jeans, with sharp features, a huge smile, and a silver buzz cut. His office was bright and organized. It did not look like we'd be blowing the dust off any scraggly texts.

I asked Steger to give me a quick summary of the science of purpose and meaning (which sounds like multiple levels of oxymoron), and he explained the foundation set in the 1940s by Viktor Frankl, an Austrian neurologist, psychiatrist, and Holocaust survivor who wrote *Man's Search for Meaning*, which was designated as one of the ten most influential books in the United States by the Library of Congress in 1991. Frankl spent three years as a prisoner in concentration camps, putting his previous vocation to use as a counselor for fellow prisoners dealing with shock, grief, and suicidal thoughts. He observed that those who found meaning even in the worst conditions were more resilient than those who didn't.

"Everything can be taken from a man but one thing," Frankl writes. "The last of the human freedoms—to choose one's attitude in any given set of circumstances, to choose one's own way."[5]

By the time he was released, he had suffered immensely, and his wife, parents, and brother, who had been taken with him, had died. When he returned to Vienna, his experience informed his approach to psychological healing, and he argued that our most primary motivational force is not to feel pleasure or avoid pain, but rather what he termed *will to meaning*: to find meaning in our lives. This informed his development of *logotherapy—logos* is a Greek word for "meaning"—which focuses on the individual's ability to determine for himself what makes life meaningful.[6]

Because Frankl considers meaning in specific (rather than abstract or general) terms, he describes meaning in life as always changing, but constant in that it's found in one of three ways: by doing or creating, by having an experience or encounter with someone or something, or by the attitude we take toward suffering. Frankl challenges the American mind-set that centers around our pursuit of happiness: "Happiness cannot be pursued; it must ensue. One must have a reason to 'be happy.'"[7]

This perspective might be jarring to people in a culture where "pursuit of happiness" is considered an unalienable right. But the results of Steger's first big project reinforced Frankl's message. Steger created his "Meaning in Life" questionnaire to measure two things: a person's *Presence of Meaning*, which indicates meaning has been discovered or understood, and *Search for Meaning*, which is a process (rather than a state). There are four possible outcomes for the scoring: high in one and low in the other, or the same in both.

Steger had predicted that people who were actively searching for meaning would be happiest ("What's more important in life than the search for meaning" he said), but the data showed that people who are happiest score high in Presence of Meaning and *low* in Search for Meaning, which inspired a flurry of subsequent articles and research correcting a popular misconception that searching for meaning is *not* the same as searching for happiness; in fact, there may be a trade-off between the two.[8]

Understanding the differences between happiness and meaning can be helpful in the day-to-day challenges we face as parents, especially considering that parents of young children report that their lives are high in meaning but not necessarily happiness.[9] When we decide to prioritize meaning over happiness (and recognize this as a choice we're making), we can help our children shape the skills they'll need to find their own meaning and purpose. In 2013, a research team led by Roy Baumeister determined key differences between the two: happiness, they found, is oriented around the present while meaningfulness integrates the past, present, and future. Happiness is concerned with meeting one's wants and needs while meaningfulness is concerned with personal identity and expression. Levels of stress, worry, and anxiety are lower in happiness and higher in meaningfulness. And finally, what I keyed in on during my talk with Steger, happiness is linked with being a "taker" while meaningfulness is linked with being a "giver."[10]

"In general," Steger says, "if we can achieve the best that we do, then our effort is, in part, going towards benefiting other people or contributing to something bigger than ourselves."

This understanding that, ultimately, a meaningful life is one that transcends the self has roots in Frankl's work: "The more one forgets himself—by giving himself to a cause to serve or another person to love—the more human he is," he writes.[11]

Comparing it to happiness gives me a good sense of what meaning is *not*, but I still needed Steger to clarify what meaning in life *is*. His initial answer wasn't very helpful: "Having a meaningful life," he said, "means that you think your life is meaningful. No more, no less."

However, he explained, because it is such a broad, umbrella term, researchers are working toward a unified definition of meaning that includes three specific components: *purpose, coherence,* and *significance.*[12] Even though we often refer to meaning and purpose as if they are interchangeable, researchers consider purpose as one *part* of meaning. Another way I think of purpose is having a vision: asking what our core goals or aspirations are in life that provide the motivation, reason, or explanation for the way we spend our time. A sense of purpose provides direction, like a guiding light, or, as Steger puts it, "an anchor we throw out into the future," helping us persevere through one moment for the sense of achievement ahead.

That I experienced such a *lack* of purpose explains my mental state after so much time on bedrest, when I missed feeling useful and contributing in ways that resonate, desperate to know when I might recover. It also explains what my children gained. Having a specific, tangible purpose transformed their list of chores from an annoying inconvenience to a meaningful contribution that they not only embraced but also took pride in doing.

Coherence can also be understood as comprehension or understanding—the ability to link moments, people, and events together in ways that make sense. We have coherence when we reply "So *that's* why . . ." to explanations and clarifications. We understand ourselves as characters in a larger setting, with a role to play in the context of what is around us, behind us, ahead of us. Steger explains that our brains have evolved to find patterns, associations, maps, and meaning everywhere.

"The question isn't 'can we find meaning in life?' We can't *not* find meaning."

Finally, significance comes from understanding that our lives are of value and importance—that they matter beyond the trivial or momentary. Significance is that intrinsic awareness I realized as an adolescent that my existence is of value beyond measure. Religions certainly have their own way to offer a sense of significance, but, Steger says, almost all of the world is a framework that can be used in this way. Like studies in awe, studies in meaning show that relationships and connections with other people are the most common source, with the natural world regularly referenced as another. Everyday ways our children feel part of something larger are all around them, in the classroom, the family, and the community. Traditions and rituals can have a powerful influence on a child's sense of connection, whether it's those they help shape or those that have been in place before they came around.

Understanding the differences in these three qualities helps me make sense of the transformation I saw in my children the summer I spent on bedrest. While I was stuck in my room questioning my own purpose and significance, the challenges they faced fulfilled what Steger describes as natural desires in children: to feel they contribute to a higher purpose; to know they fit into something bigger; to be assured that their lives are significant enough that they can make a positive impact.

As for coherence—making sense of the way our summer unfolded—I got that one. If there's one thing I can do, it's turn anything into a story.

History and definitions aside, I want to understand more about how the science of purpose and meaning helps me as a parent. After all, like moral reasoning, the search for and discovery of meaning comes from an intrinsic motivation. I can nurture qualities in my kids that might be helpful, but Steger is firm as he reminds me that the search for meaning is an extremely personal, intimate endeavor. Frankl writes that this uniqueness is what gives each individual life such value: "He cannot be replaced, nor can his life be repeated."[13]

And like morality, meaning is more of a practice or journey rather than a goal or destination. What's so different from my childhood understanding is that meaning can change as life changes; it's not something we have to settle on but continue to look for at each turn. So, while no one can give meaning to anyone else, as a practice, there are certain skills we can encourage in our children as they grow. Those components of meaning—significance, coherence, and purpose—are ideas we can affirm and reaffirm to a child over time, Steger says: your life is precious; you have an ability to figure out what this world is like; you have a way to fit in.

The "why" questions children and teens are so prone to asking are a way they are working to understand these things. Instead of dismissing the questions or offering quick answers, we can encourage our kids to keep at it, to nurture an exploration of their inner lives. It can be difficult at *any* age to be in touch with what we most want from life rather than what others want from us or what is expected. We can encourage our children to practice introspection, to reflect on the values, strengths, and passions they have, by asking big questions and listening deeply to their answers: What are your favorite things to do? What are you good at? What do you like about your closest friends? What are things that make you angry or sad? What are ways you help other people? What makes you feel really good? What makes you feel really bad?

As children begin to develop a strong sense of self, they will also be observing the rest of the world, trying to make sense of how it works and where their place is in it. A win-win for everyone involved is that we make sure they are active, collaborative players in their own lives, starting right in the home. Even the youngest children are capable of contributing around the house, at school, and in the community. The twins' first experience with preschool opened my eyes to how much more they were capable of than I realized. Not only did the whole class contribute to their environment by setting the table for snacks, pouring drinks, and putting away their toys, but they were also thrilled to do it once they understood that everyone has a way to pitch in. The rural community we've settled in is relatively isolated, but once a year it hosts a Labor Day Art Fair. The sign-up for children's volunteer slots opens months in advance as the kids in the community anticipate their jobs selling popcorn, clearing food trays, wiping down tables. The pride and sense of accomplishment they experience is palpable during the three full days they dedicate to working hard and keeping busy.

Steger points out that, just as we have evolved to seek coherence, finding patterns and associations all around us, we have an intrinsic "need to do," the result of evolving from active species, always on the move to "seek and obtain what we need in life."

A challenging juxtaposition to this "need to do" (and one that's equally valuable) is that we also allow time for idleness. Those still moments in our children's lives—the ones often accompanied by the dreaded words *I'm bored*—force them to reconcile with big, uncomfortable, crucial questions that will remain with them for a lifetime. I think of what meaning boils down to for me—a knowing that the way I spend my time is intentional—and realize my children won't know how to do this if they are never given a chance to practice.

As tempting as it is for parents to step in and address boredom as though it's a problem to be solved, we can embrace unstructured time for our kids as a way for them to make decisions about how *they* want to spend their time, with as little outside interference or entertainment as possible. In a culture where we equate "being busy" with worth and success, it's easy to forget that our children need moments in life quiet enough to hear themselves, to get to know their hearts and minds. Moving from one packed hour to the next, or relying on someone or something else for entertainment, doesn't allow children to practice looking inside for direction, an invaluable skill in the search for purpose and meaning.

When we put it in perspective, dealing with boredom is one of the *least* painful challenges our kids will have to navigate in their lives. As Frankl observed, our approach to inevitable suffering is one of the most meaningful ways we find meaning. We often have more agency than we sometimes believe to address our problems or change our circumstances, but, Frankl writes, "When we are no longer able to change a situation . . . we are challenged to change ourselves."[14]

Indeed, it's often when we suffer, or witness the suffering of others, that we begin to question meaning in the first place, asking *Why?* and *What can I do?* Whether one subscribes to a worldview that insists God has a plan or a worldview that insists there is no plan (or something in between), we are all trying to make sense of injustice, unfairness, and suffering in life. And like nurturing the inner self and understanding how we fit into the world around us, learning to make sense of suffering takes practice. As parents, we can encourage our children to reflect on what they gain from suffering: things such as strength, resiliency, empathy, compassion, humility. Witnessing the suffering of others can motivate them to take action, to put their skills and passions to use for a cause greater than themselves.

Finally, especially as our children mature, we can help them find ways to break out of the mold of everyday life. Research in neuroscience and developmental psychology reaffirms what many of us have experienced ourselves and suspect in our children: the adolescent brain is unique from the child or adult brain in its drive to seek novelty and take risks.[15] While this natural progression presents a frightening set of challenges for parents, there's also good reason for it. Teenagers are working toward greater independence and self-discovery, integrating the old with the new to forge their own identities. We can encourage our children to break from the routine in ways that expand their perspectives, offering new ways to understand themselves and engage in the world.

I think of the perspective shift I experienced as a teenager on that class trip to the Rocky Mountains in Colorado. I experienced a recalibration in my understanding of how vast and majestic this world is; it triggered my lifelong desire to travel, a passion to care for and protect the environment, a thirst to learn more about how other people live; it ignited a spark of hope in my insecure, adolescent self that out there, somewhere in the world, I might find a place I felt at home. These types of experiences—travel, spending time outdoors, serving others, meeting new people, or experiencing a change in circumstance—are all opportunities for our children to gain a sense of purpose, coherence, and significance as they make their way toward living a meaningful life.

The thing that stands out to me most about Michael Steger is his easy assertion that we find meaning, at least in part, by helping others in a tangible way. When I asked him to tell me about his personal history leading to this work, it was clear that from the time he was a child he wanted to make a positive impact on the world. Where, I wondered, did that come from?

"My parents," he replied, with no hesitation. "They modeled it for me. Mom taught English to refugees. My dad ran a community health center."

When he said this, I thought of another study I'd run into while looking into connections between children and purpose, a 2014 report titled "The Children We Mean to Raise." A team from the Harvard Graduate School of Education surveyed more than ten thousand middle and high school students across a wide spectrum of races, cultures, and classes, asking them to rank values such as achievement, happiness, and caring for others. The study found that 80 percent of those surveyed valued aspects of personal success over concern for others. These were not only the students' priorities: 80 percent believe their parents *also* prioritize their achievement and personal happiness over caring for others.[16]

But what was so strange—indeed, the inspiration for the report's title—is that the student responses are not commensurate with the adults' responses to the same questions. The team also surveyed parents and teachers, who responded that having caring children is their priority, which is clearly at odds with what their children are taking away. The authors suggest that this discrepancy between what parents prioritize and what their children *think* they prioritize is due to what they term a *rhetoric/reality gap*, a gap between what parents and other adults say are their top priorities and the real messages they convey in their behavior day to day.[17]

Steger didn't hesitate in pointing to his parents as altruistic influences on his work, a worthy goal for any parent who wants to close the rhetoric/reality gap. I don't mean to paint a romantic, idealized, or unattainable picture of what a meaningful life looks like; we don't need to drop everything we're doing and relocate across the globe as disaster-relief volunteers. It's not *what* we are doing so much as *why* and whether we're doing it intentionally, consciously participating in our own lives. For one of his studies, Steger gave a group of students disposable cameras and had them photograph things throughout their days that gave their lives meaning. They included a brief write-up to go along with the images. The one that stands out most to me is a photograph of a man emptying a trash can in the student common center. Steger points out that this is a scene constantly playing out in public spaces around us; it may seem mundane, but the intent behind the action can always lead to something profound.

"Though I am a custodian, I am proud to be one," the man writes. "I am proud because the job pays for my family."

Everything this person needs to live a meaningful life—purpose, coherence, significance—is right there. We may not always see it in one another, but we're expressing our values by the way we spend our time. And whether we're conscious of it or not, we're always making trade-offs: when we choose to spend time doing one thing, we're also choosing *not* to do another. I heard an expression recently that captures this point with a retake on an old cliché: the grass is always greener, not on the other side, *but where you water it.*

When I asked Steger if our family might be missing something about meaning and purpose by not being religious, he pointed out that religious teachings are explicit in what they're saying about values and what it means to be a good person. Religious organizations are well known for their efforts in philanthropy, charity, and giving. Without this organized framework in place, Steger points out, "we can also, as parents, be very explicit about the things that we care about and think are correct, in terms of saying what the world is like and how to be a good person, which is what meaning and purpose try to express."

The rhetoric/reality gap reminds me that it's not enough to just *talk* about our values, and I turn to the great human equalizer, our hours in a day, to consider whether the way we live our lives expresses those values. In a disconcerting way, I've realized that simply taking a glimpse at the family calendar will tell me what I want to know. And the truth is, they don't always line up the way I would like to think they do. I see chunks of time dedicated to work, school, and domesticity; practices, games, and lessons; trips, excursions, and adventures. I'm not seeing much blocked off in the way of service to others. And if *I* don't make service and giving a priority, no one else is going to do it for me.

This awareness is, perhaps, part of the reason that someone with high scores in Search for Meaning will also report feelings of anxiousness or unease about life. As a teenager, I used to think that once the big, assumed midlife questions were answered—marriage, children, career—I might understand my place in the world and feel at peace with how I spend my days. Now I'm in the middle of living those answers and still find myself asking *What's the point?* not just for myself but also for four other people.

But I also find peace in knowing that asking *What's the point?* might just *be* the point, at least for me, and it will probably be something different for my kids. This is a concept Steger finds himself clarifying often: He can tell us *how* to think about meaning and *where* to look for it and *why* it's important. But he can't answer *what* it is for anyone else. That's the difficult and rewarding part each of us must determine for ourselves, and what makes meaning so meaningful.

It's true that, like a moral compass, we can't *hand* our values to our children; we can't *hand* them a meaningful life. But we are their first teachers. We can make the effort to pinpoint our own values, to be mindful that how we spend our time expresses those values, and model for our children that a meaningful life—one that integrates self-understanding with contribution to a need outside of the self, being a "giver" rather than a "taker"—is something worth striving for.

THREE COMPONENTS OF MEANING IN LIFE

- *Purpose*: A sense of purpose is having a reason for doing the things we do. Purpose provides direction, like a guiding light, or, as Steger puts it, "an anchor we throw out into the future," helping us persevere through one moment for the sense of achievement ahead.
- *Comprehension*: Comprehension is our ability to make sense of things. We have coherence when we reply "So *that's* why . . ." to explanations and clarifications. We understand ourselves as characters in a larger

setting, with a role to play in the context of what is around us, behind us, ahead of us.

- *Significance*: Significance is understanding our life's worth. We gain a sense of significance when we know that our lives are of value and importance—that they matter beyond the trivial or momentary.

HELPING CHILDREN AND TEENS CULTIVATE A SENSE OF PURPOSE AND MEANING

- *Nourish the inner life*: A meaningful life transcends the self, but it begins with understanding the self. Encourage children to think about who they are, what they stand for, and what they're good at. Ask questions about values, strengths, passions. Things that make them angry, sad, and frustrated provide opportunities for further self-discovery as well.
- *Encourage contribution and collaboration*: We all have a drive to participate, to get involved, and feel a sense of significance when we have a job to do. Children of all ages can participate in their daily lives. Establishing routines, rituals, and traditions that include our children gives them a great sense of purpose, coherence, and significance.
- *Allow for stillness*: When we are too busy rushing from one thing to the next or distracting ourselves with forms of entertainment, we forget how to listen to the mind and the heart. Let children have the practice to make decisions about how they spend their time in ways that don't rely on being entertained by someone or something else.
- *Provide perspective in suffering*: Suffering in life is inevitable; one of the most valuable gifts we can give our children is practice in navigating it. Viktor Frankl writes, "In some ways suffering ceases to be suffering at the moment it finds a meaning," which means it's not the circumstance that changes to alleviate suffering but the way the mind makes sense of the circumstance.[18]
- *Provide opportunities for new experiences*: When we follow the same routine each day, we may become complacent or switch on autopilot. Adolescents, especially, seek novel experiences and enjoy taking risks. Encourage this drive and provide ways for them to broaden their per-

spectives. Experiences such as travel, spending time outdoors, serving others, meeting new people, or experiencing a change in circumstance are all opportunities for our children to gain a sense of purpose, coherence, and significance as they make their way toward living a meaningful life.

INTERLUDE:
PALO ALTO

I was thirty years old, married with three young kids, and fresh out of grad school in the Midwest with no plan for what was next. Chris and I faced a question that had hovered over us like a cloud since we met: Is now the time to move? When mutual friends introduced us six years prior, we'd bonded immediately over our dreams of exploration, of getting out of town, which we put on hold quickly when I got pregnant with twins. At the time, my mom was our next-door neighbor and Chris's parents were not far, a manageable drive south. We both had aunts, uncles, and cousins nearby. We both had sisters in town. We had a tight circle of friends. We may have been naive regarding what having twins would entail, but at least we knew it was not the time to kick off some wanderlust adventure and move away from a built-in support system.

It's not that either of us didn't love where we lived in Kansas; in fact, our loyalty was part of the dilemma. We'd each found our way there independently of one another because of the university, and the eclectic, vibrant, progressive culture—locals call it the "oasis on the plains"—keeps many graduates local long after their commencement ceremonies. We were among this group of intentional townies and met when we were both working, paying off debt, and thinking about a next step. We may have spent time poring over maps together, but we loved plenty about Kansas: the wide open spaces, the slower pace, the thunderstorms and sunsets.

When we had the twins and, later, our daughter, we relied heavily on the support of others. Even though we eventually bought a home across town from my mom, she still helped us on a regular basis. We spent holidays with Chris's family. We spent summer evenings and college game days with friends, none of whom had kids yet but folded ours into the group like family. Several of my peers in grad school were also young parents, living in student-family housing, running to the campus childcare center, juggling teaching, studying, and parenting in the same sort of manic frenzy as me. The way our lives were unfolding hadn't been predicted or planned, but having the stability of relationships and rituals with family, friends, and community gave us a cohesiveness, a sense of contained chaos, like butterflies in a net. We were safe . . . but then, we wanted to get out and explore a little further.

This is when the opportunity came up, through Chris's job, for us to move to California. *Why not?* we thought. I was done with grad school, the twins were ready for elementary school, and having one baby seemed like a piece of cake compared to surviving the first several years with two. We felt that the reinforcements we'd had in Kansas had propped us up when we needed it, but it seemed like we were ready to set out on that adventure we'd put on hold before becoming a family of five.

I grew up moving regularly and wasn't daunted by what was ahead. My memories of moving as a child are positive; I don't know if it was just my nature or a child's way of adapting, but I viewed it as an adventure, full of promise. And whenever we did move, one of the first things my mom did was locate the church we would attend. Even though we didn't know anyone when we arrived in town, finding a church instantly surrounded us with the type of resources and support a family needs in a new place.

Of all the practical details we had to square away for the move—selling our home in Kansas, finding a rental in California, transporting our things, enrolling the kids in school, getting ourselves across the country—we missed an important one that we relied on in the Midwest and what my mom knew to find in churches: connections with other people. Of all places for a family to land without any relationships in place, Silicon Valley has got to be one of the more difficult. While older residents in the Bay Area Peninsula assure me that it's not what it used to be, several decades of tech booms have created an environment notorious for the way its residents are compartmentalized and isolated, both from one another and from the outside world. Companies such as Apple, Facebook, and Google have created campuses bigger than most towns I've lived in, where employees can eat, sleep, work out, and get their laundry done without needing to leave the premises.

I was not ready for this. Because people living in Silicon Valley are rarely *from* Silicon Valley, other families we met through the school were making similar transitions, and we tended to stick together. This was some connection, a way to soften our landing, but not the kind that felt rooted in something deeper, more timeless than simply having children the same age. When I think of the community we'd left behind, I think of people of various ages, lifestyles, backgrounds, and interests. The diversity was crucial, as it allowed for alternating and reciprocating support in hard times. When I think of the extended family we'd left behind, I think of long-standing traditions and rituals and a collective identity that transcends the sum of its parts. I wanted to feel the relief of being enfolded into something that's been going long before my arrival and will continue to churn after I depart. My mom had found these things through the church, but where could we look? Without religion, how can we find the connection, rituals, and support that we need?

7.

FAMILY

Growing apart doesn't change the fact that for a long time we grew side by side; our roots will always be tangled.

—Ally Condie

The summer our sons were freshly six and our daughter was not yet two, we moved across the country, from Kansas to California. Like having a baby or losing someone you love, a big move is one of those events that irrevocably changes your life, the kind of event that, when you look back, creates a timeline reference for "before" and "after." At least, we suspected this would be true and planned to give the transition some gravity by stretching the journey west over two weeks. Chris and I are both minimalist types, in that we are more at ease with less stuff around, so we looked forward to sending our belongings off with a moving company (by the time we were packed, we half hoped we'd never see them again) and carrying only camping essentials and three kids in the minivan for our cross-country drive.

That two-week period was so full of novelty and adventure and big feelings that it exists in our minds as a lifetime of its own. Everyone but the baby was crying as we pulled out of the town where Chris and I had gone through college, started working, met, married, had children, and owned a home. It was bittersweet, to leave a tight group of friends, good neighbors, and family contained in a close radius and head for a place of amazing natural beauty where Chris had a secure job but where we knew absolutely no one.

As we traveled, the collective mood in the van shifted from grief through the heartland to elation at the Rockies, an alien detachment in out-of-the-way Yellowstone, a foreboding through Nevada, and, finally, a buzzing anticipation as we approached the coast.

We pulled into Palo Alto, a Silicon Valley suburb forty minutes south of San Francisco, after two weeks of living out of the van and camping in national parks. We were modern-day Beverly Hillbillies, a big Midwestern brood arriving in California, smelling like campfire with dirt between our toes. It was surreal, going from such wild environments, an unfettered pace, and intensive togetherness to quintessential suburban life, with its curated lawns, tight schedules, and, as soon as Chris headed out for his first day of work, a sudden cloud of domestic isolation.

When I pictured living in California before our move, I pictured the tourist's version of California, an endless beach vacation. I got the same reaction every time I told people where I was from: *You're not in Kansas anymore!* But what I discovered was that everyday life is everyday life, even when it's sunny and 72 degrees. As if we were getting what we asked for, our moving van was several weeks late. I was taking care of three young children in an empty rental house, save for a broken refrigerator and overflowing toilets. We were working with whatever clothes and supplies we had from the drive. This was not California Dreamin': there were groceries that needed to be bought, diapers that needed to be changed, and traffic that needed to be sat in. One of Chris's coworkers, who'd been through a similar relocation process, graciously offered their washer and dryer (and usually ended up feeding us for good measure). Going over to a stranger's home to do laundry turned into the highlight of our week.

As I started piecing together where to go for gasoline, toilet paper, and flip flops and stood in lines for school enrollment, a drivers' license, and stamps, I realized how much context—or, as my mom put it once when I was younger, "timing"—affects our budding relationships and reactions to our environment. Knowing we were in California to stay, at least for a while, made the people and places around me take different shape than they would if I were just passing through. I tried harder to make sense of them, to relate to them, to understand my place among them. I wasn't the only one: the allure of possibility in California and the harsh reality that it's not for everyone means people are always coming and going. Another family might have been able to find the connection I was looking for at a nearby church, but this wasn't an option. Day in and day out, the awareness that I didn't know anyone around me intensified. I felt incredibly lonely and desperately confused. Having no sort of personal connections to relate with had me feeling as if I didn't know who *I* was, either.

Not long after we arrived to our new town, I decided to get out of it. For reasons that are mostly unconnected and not simple, I have three siblings who made California their home state years before us: my older half-brothers and their families are spread out in the LA area, about six hours south. Though I underestimated how big the state actually is, I moved to California hoping to reconnect with them as much as possible. The youngest of the three is still seven years older than me, and we grew up always in different stages of life. As a group, we operate with a sort of "out of sight, out of mind" attitude; we are intensely present with one another in person but don't make many efforts to connect when we're apart. And we'd been apart for quite some time.

The first chance we got, the kids and I loaded back up in the van and headed south; the six-hour drive was small potatoes compared to our recent six-state drive. I'm not sure what I was expecting, if I was expecting anything. I hadn't seen my siblings in several years, and we'd all gone through changes. We needed to catch up and get to know one another's families; in total, we have twelve kids, some of whom had not yet met. But the reunion was incredibly joyous. After months of such intense transition—the packing, the voyage, the relocation—being with my siblings made me finally feel *home* again. It wasn't about our physical location; just being in a room with them reminded me *this is where I'm from.* It's telling, I think, that we call family members "relatives." After feeling so alone in a new place, I was looking to *relate with* and ground myself *in relation to* people who've known me from the beginning. The Latin origin for "relate" is *referre*, which means "to bring back" or "to bear," which, in turn, means "to hold or support." I was looking for my siblings to bring me back; I was looking to them for support.

I watched as our children merged into a roaming pack that reminded me of my own childhood with cousins, running unrestrained and looking to any adult who might care for them: shove a bite of sandwich here, stop and blow your nose there. I felt it again in my bones, that primal childhood elation of experiencing such freedom and security together—being part of a herd. My children had an immediate connection with their cousins and cried when it was time to go, the same way I did when I was a child.

I returned to the Bay Area from that first visit south a little surer, a little more confident about forging ahead with this new life we were creating. I also kept going back to see my siblings. Being in my brother's home, with our children together, felt like glimpses of a lighthouse after weeks spent drifting unmoored. We must have made the six-hour drive south at least half a dozen times our first year in California. As time passed, though, things slowly changed: our nuclear family began establishing new friendships, creating new routines, becoming more familiar with the area. We were con- structing our own little lighthouse, and, after about a year, we noticed the first time we felt "back home" after a visit south.

At some undetermined point, I shifted from wanting to be with my sib- lings after too long without them to wanting to return home after too long with my siblings. I had needed them for connection and support during this transition, and by providing that, they helped me need them less. This is one of the things families do. After five years in the Bay Area, three sketchy rentals, and eventually our own home, we don't make the drive south so frequently now, so desperately, but we still reunite a few times a year, for holidays or school vacations. And no matter how long my kids go without seeing their cousins, they pick up right where they left off.

Despite some mishaps and complications along the way, this type of connection with extended family is what I want for my kids and for myself. I think about my own connections as a child—with my siblings, cousins, aunts, uncles, grandparents—I felt so intertwined with all of them that I understood myself as a small detail contained in a larger, colorful tapestry. Even now, with this group of people spread across the country, involved in our own diverse and sometimes conflicting interests and lifestyles, I still know my place within my family better than I know it anywhere else. For better *and* worse, I forever hear echoes of the voices from my past, voices of the people who bear witness to my life.

It's that shared history that defines "family" for me, not necessarily bio- logical status. I can't count the number of times I've showed up for a holiday, reunion, or wedding and greeted a person I'd never seen before. No one on my mother's side of the family thought twice about including coworkers, acquaintances, and neighbors in our gatherings. A fair number of our family albums contain exchange students and friends, smiling next to a bride or un-wrapping a present. Some synonyms for the word "adopt" are *embrace* and *accept*. As a group, we like to adopt. A few of my friends have been included as a part of my family for so long that our relationships resemble those of siblings: our shared interests, worldviews, and lifestyles may diverge at times, but the sheer longevity of our connection to one another forever ties us. It's the names of these people—the ones who've known me the longest, not necessarily the best—that flash through my mind in my darkest times of need, no matter how long it's been since we've spoken.

It wasn't until I was older and observed the way some families take pride in their exclusivity that I realized just how welcoming my own was, a par-ticular value I didn't realize was a value until later in life. It's a legacy my sib-lings and I still embrace, with at least one person (and usually a few) around at our gatherings who may not have another place to go. Without explicitly doing so, family life establishes these types of values that help shape our identities and a sense of how we operate in the larger world. It's true that many members of my extended family are deeply religious; it's also true that as a group they value sincerity, adaptation, and inclusion over almost any-thing else. The value of a close family itself is something I took for granted as a given growing up, until I met others who had a different experience.

There's a cultural decline in having extended family nearby because of circumstances like ours: in 2015, the Census Bureau estimated that, due to factors like education and job opportunities, affordable housing, and mar-riage, the average American will move eleven times in her life.[1] American families are becoming more mobile and dispersed with each generation. But even when we are unable to remain physically close to one another, there are plenty of reasons to prioritize our rooted relationships, as challenging as this can sometimes be. Some anthropologists describe us as "cooperative breeders," which means we have evolved to raise our children in groups, supporting one another in mind and spirit, if not always in body.[2] This benefits parents as well as children. Decades of research in psychology, sociology, and child development shows that family environments that em-phasize closeness and support for one another contribute to a child's social and emotional well-being.

Seeing my own children's bond with their cousins, aunts, uncles, and grandparents reminds me of what it feels like, in the midst of the wild jungles of childhood, to *know* that there is a network of people who love and care for me unconditionally. When I needed a break from my own parents—or they needed a break from me—there were other adults I could turn to. With several generations and differences in age spanning every decade, no stage of life was mysterious or unknown; I observed it all. Being so unconditionally connected to such a large, diverse group showed me that some of the more difficult challenges people face in life—divorce, addiction, poverty, abuse, mental illness—can happen to anyone.

As often as we moved, the assurance that my mother's extended family was always available—at least a few times a year in person and always by phone or mail—provided a sense of security and stability that I wouldn't have had otherwise. When adolescence crept in and I began to swell with self-doubt and insecurity, the same people who loved me through my childhood were still there, reminding me that the love doesn't change just because I was changing. Through early adulthood and a storm of experiments and bad decisions, my extended family never allowed me to doubt my sense of worth. They have since welcomed my husband and children with the same open arms.

That type of longevity for any relationship requires working through difficulties. For as much goodness as we've offered one another, we have also managed to inflict pain. Of the many benefits being part of a close family offers, constant happiness is not one of them. Some of us are so incredibly different, I can't imagine that this group of people would actively *choose* to be connected if we weren't related, which is exactly what makes it an important kind of relationship to manage. It's because of the inevitable conflicts that arise that we—and our children—learn more about perspective, empathy, and resilience. If we can find grace, patience, and understanding within our extended families, the rest of the world might seem a little less overwhelming.

Out in California, my siblings and I are (somewhat clumsily) re-creating what we had as children, a network of aunts and uncles, nieces and nephews, and a few adopted extras, with a quick make-up of beds and stock-up on groceries because *The cousins are coming!* We get together and retell stories from our pasts, laughing, arguing, and interrupting one another to get them straight, no matter how many times they've been told. We learn new things about one another, realize that we've interpreted and experienced events differently, with individual inner lives that are sometimes taken for granted in the larger framework of family life. I'm guessing our children absorb some of this on the periphary, attempting to catalog us adults with hushed labels, as I did as a child: "the funny one," "the wild one," "my favorite one." Maybe they use the stories we tell to make sense of who we are and, eventually, will use them to help make sense of who *they* are.

These sorts of stories our children absorb over the years about their families make a difference in how they navigate the rest of the world. In his *New York Times* article "The Stories That Bind Us," author and father Bruce Feiler points to a study done by psychologists at Emory University to encourage readers to consciously think about their family narratives. The research team was interested in how to counteract the effects of our increasingly dissipating American families. Psychologist Marshall Duke led a study in which children from four dozen families answered twenty "Do you know?" questions about their families: where their grandparents grew up, how their parents met, and when their family faced hardship, for example.[3]

After a number of other psychological tests and observations over a time period that included the immediate post-9/11 window, the team concluded that children who knew more about their family's history had higher self-esteem and were more resilient. Dr. Duke credits the results with what he calls the child's "intergenerational self," which, like experiencing awe and being part of a community, gives them the understanding that they are part of something larger than themselves. "The 'Do You Know?' scale," Feiler writes, "turned out to be the best single predictor of children's emotional health and happiness."[4]

They are listening not only to the content of the family narratives but also to the way we present the content—the "spin," if you will, with the most effective being what Dr. Duke calls the "oscillating" family narrative: the one that explores the ups *and* downs.

I'm guessing, too, that our kids pick up on the things we *don't* talk about. As per usual recommendations, my siblings and I generally avoid discussing religion, politics, and complicated social issues over the holiday table. In some ways, we are a group of aunts and uncles I remember from my childhood: all are religious except my husband and me, and, even though this generation doesn't emphasize religiosity as vocally, our status as nonbelievers still seems to hang out there.

I suppose this makes me the adult I was wary of and confused by: the Atheist Aunt. I don't feel great about this because the only thing that my aunt's status as a nonbeliever meant to me as a child was that I needed to pray for her, which turned her into an object more than a person I could know, with her own ideas, thoughts, and opinions. Even though I am closer to her now, I regret that I held her apart in my mind when I was young: there were my regular aunts and uncles, all known and available and whole, and then there was . . . The Atheist. Mysterious, unknowable, incomplete. It was clear to me that I mustn't ask her about religion, and it seemed clear to her that she mustn't talk about it.

This sort of *don't-ask-don't-tell* approach seems to be a family pattern that is hard to break. When adults can't model ways to openly explore and understand differences in belief, children learn not to. It's only polite sometimes that we keep this information to ourselves, and there are worse ways to handle religious differences, but it also feels like a loss that I can't be entirely known by the people who remind me *this is where I'm from.*

Experiencing that sense of loss due to difference in belief within families can be heartbreaking, and it permeates relationships in a number of ways. For people who sincerely believe that religion is a matter of life and death, that belief determines where our souls spend eternity, the cognitive dissonance required to show support for nonbelievers in their families is tremendous. For the rest of us, just differing worldviews or the knowledge that we're working against stereotypes can be deterring, whether we want to avoid being pegged as the combative, detached atheist or the disapproving, prudish person of faith. Sometimes it's just easier to drop the eye contact, clear the table, and start working on the dishes.

But my own experience—and the research—shows that, as much as there is to work through, having a close extended family is something to strive for. And just to be clear, as much as I value a close extended family, I've come to understand that family is *many* things, but it can't be *everything*. This is an important disclosure for me to make. There's nothing wrong with acknowledging that no one person, or group of people, can be *all* things to another. The simple, yet painful, step of acknowledging that sense of loss helps me make room for what we can be.

When we're considering a group of people who've known one another for as long as family members do, it can be difficult *not* to paint each other with broad strokes, to think we know all because we know one, or that we know the person in the present because we knew the person in the past. And sometimes the ones who are the most outspoken are the ones who end up inadvertently speaking for the rest. I know some of my relatives more as individuals, but others I know more as part of a category: "the uncles" or "the super-religious ones" or "the ones in Indiana." It's for this reason that things individual family members have done or said that hurt me have affected the way I perceive and feel perceived by the rest of the group.

Shortly after I'd become a mother, an aunt I hadn't seen in almost a decade was visiting for Christmas. One evening, in the soft glow of holiday lights, we found a moment together on the sofa. She cuddled my son in her arms, looked in my eyes, and abruptly declared with an uncanny mixture of sweetness and foreboding that I wouldn't meet my babies in heaven if I didn't raise them in Christ.

I was an emotional, anxious new mother, as women in my generation tend to be, and this did not sit well with me. Her words instantly took me through flashbacks of my religious upbringing, like a slippery ride through a tunnel—the confusion, guilt, and pain of leaving—a ride she had no idea I'd taken. I want to spare my children this journey. I love my aunt (one of "the super-religious ones"), and I knew, in *her* mind, she was saying the right thing, but during this particular Yuletide chat I nodded my head politely and determined right then and there that no one in my family would talk to my kids about religion.

The way I reacted to my aunt's words covered *any* relation, from my long-distance second cousin's stepsister to my own mother, without consideration or exception. No one in my beloved, maddening extended family would talk to my children about religion. This was an easy enough goal to achieve before my children could speak. But then one night over spaghetti, when our sons were three, one of them asked "Who is God?" after spending the day with my mom. She had told him "God is everywhere" and, remembering a talk we'd had earlier about germs, he wondered if God was like bacteria.

This was a great question, a fun question, but one I missed in the moment because I reacted emotionally, with irritation and anger. Because I've always fallen onto the "free range" parenting side of the spectrum more than "helicopter," this desire to control and limit my children's religious exposure was peculiar and, in retrospect, a pretty obvious sign that I needed to work out some issues. It's one thing to have a brief encounter with friends or family we see once in a decade. It's another to face this issue on a regular basis. My mom and I—even though we were living in the same town and seeing one another almost daily—had not talked about religion in years. She knew Chris and I didn't go to church, and that was about it. Likewise, it's been obvious to me that her spiritual life has evolved since I was a child. Yet when I heard that she'd mentioned the word *God* to my kids, I assumed she would tell them the same things she told me thirty years ago. In some cases, maybe this would be a correct assumption. In most cases, it's not. My emotional reaction blinded me from seeing that, in the same way my religious aunt hadn't allowed for *my* change and growth, I wasn't allowing for my mother's.

Somehow, that evening, I was able to contain this reaction mostly to my mind (though body language usually gives away enough). After what felt like a few very long moments, with Chris just sort of . . . waiting, I told my son the thing I most wished I would have heard as a child: "Well, *some* people say God is everywhere."

And that simple phrase helped me realize there are other options between the all-or-nothing approach to religion for our kids, a factual statement delivered with as little judgment as possible. I try to remember this motto about parenting in almost every dilemma: "You can't prepare the world for your child, but you can prepare your child for the world." Religion is part of our world, something they'll need to navigate, and religion within our own extended family and other rooted relationships is a good place for them to start. And because I loathe the religious judgment I remember from my past, I'm sensitive to the fact that judgment is possible from a secular perspective and can be just as hurtful.

There's something else, too, besides using our family members' various beliefs as lessons in religious education. It was facing this dilemma head-on and having a difficult discussion with my mom (one that required that I update her on my own changes in belief—a coming out, so to speak) that helped me realize how unfair it was for me to ask her to keep that part of her life to herself. I can't have it both ways: invite family members into our lives but ask them to keep meaningful parts of themselves out. That kind of relationship is conditional. The hope for families is that our love is *unconditional*.

Belief is such a crucial component of identity for so many people I love and my children love. Asking them not to share that part of their lives with my children (or dismissing or insulting them out of earshot) would result in the same kind of distance I'd had with my mom's oldest sister, the Atheist, a woman who I've come to cherish and identify with as an adult. Many non-believers have gotten used to an unspoken rule within our families to keep our skepticism to ourselves, but reciprocating the same approach with the believers in our lives only perpetuates the problem.

Having someone in my life like Chris, whose experience and tempera-ment make him more neutral in religious matters, has helped me navigate some of these paths connecting my children to my family. For such a long time, through absorption more than a direct source, I'd only known two options for discussing religious beliefs: either you believe what everyone around you believes and vocalize it or you don't and stay quiet. But this is how we can benefit from including outsiders into the family mix: they bring new perspectives, they offer alternatives, they allow us to see one another in a new light.

It took another outsider-who-is-now-an-insider, my sister-in-law, to say something else I wish I'd heard as a child, something valuable for my own children to hear. When a headline-making social issue came up in postdin-ner conversation one night, we all attempted to wade into a murky topic. A devoutly religious person herself, she offered her opinion on the controversy with the preface, "Of course, it depends on your worldview, but . . ."

It depends on your worldview. I could barely concentrate on what she said after this. *It depends on your worldview.* Of course! Of course it does, so much so that, in an objective world where we aren't influenced by our experiences and upbringing, or when we're with strangers instead of fam-ily, this qualifying statement would go without saying. But hearing it in an environment where the child in me thought that we mustn't admit that it's possible we *have* different worldviews (or that only one is the right one) was like a fresh rush of crisp air swept through the house.

Ironically enough, it's because of the conversations I was hoping to avoid when I first became a parent that I'm less worried about what others share with my children about belief. Once I dropped my initial defensiveness, I've realized that having such religiously vocal people in my children's life can be a learning experience, for them *and* me. I know our children have the same late-night philosophical run-downs with their cousins that I remember hav-ing as a child because of the questions that come up on the drive home. It's up to me to be open enough in my answers that the questions keep coming. With each year that goes by, I've understood that I can't always control what they hear, like I thought I might when they were just babies in my arms, but I can help prepare them for what they might hear, beginning with two important points we regularly go over: (1) that they be wary if someone insists they keep a secret, and (2) that they be wary if someone insists there's only one right way to talk about God.

Of course, these are easy points to make and share with my kids when I'm living in a progressive part of the country, partnered with someone who's on the same page, and connected to extended families who, though widely varied along the religious spectrum, are ultimately, unconditionally, available for us. But I wondered, what about parents who are in different situations? While a few mishaps here and there might cause some temporary detachment within my extended family, I'm lucky to have a domestic partner with a worldview similar to my own. But I also think about how, had life worked out differently, that might not have been the case. I wanted to hear from someone who has a different story to tell, and there's one person in particular I've had in mind: one Mr. Neil Carter of Jackson, Mississippi, the man behind the blog *Godless in Dixie*.

I can't remember how, exactly, I stumbled onto Carter's blog, but I do remember *why* I kept reading long into the night after the first post. For one thing, his story is compelling and relatable, which is why the blog he began in 2013, hoping to reach a few hundred readers, has drawn up to eighty thousand during its busiest months. As a former evangelical Christian in what he calls the "Buckle of the Bible Belt," who left his faith in his midthirties, Carter has a way of writing about issues in nonbelief—of being "Godless in Dixie"—that are more nuanced and considered than almost anything I've seen. It's refreshing. As much as I learn from and appreciate the work by prominent atheist authors, I find that spending too much time in their head space can affect connections I hope to maintain with people who share my past. Because of my personal and emotional past with religion, too, I tend to feel like an outsider among outspoken nonbelievers as much as I do among outspoken believers. But Carter's writing has a balanced tone that many of us who have weathered the cultural shift away from religion must be looking for: he's confident, but not arrogant; intelligent, but not condescending;

opinionated, but flexible. Rather than being provocative or subversive, he's more interested in diplomacy and thoughtfulness in matters of belief.

Once I learned a little more about him, I understood why. Describing himself as "pathologically conciliatory," Carter was born and raised in Jackson, Mississippi, and brought up in the same First Baptist Church where his parents were married. As a teenager, he became the most outspoken believer in his family, being "born again" and baptized for a second time and embracing evangelism. He taught Sunday school, met his future wife in a ministry group, and even attended seminary for two years. He and his wife had four daughters together and, for more than a decade, one of the more enviable marriages in their church community.

Carter is careful to explain that nothing traumatic or sudden caused him to lose his faith, an assumption he runs into a lot when he talks about his deconversion. He simply stopped silencing the "inner skeptic" he describes himself as having since he was a child, something that caused him to feel as if he kept part of himself hidden in a closet. This type of language, being "in the closet" and "coming out," echoes that used by the LGBT community and is common among nonbelievers in more conservative parts of the country. The more Carter explored his skepticism, the more he felt as though he were living a double life, if only in his head. Still, though he knew that bringing up his doubt with his wife, family, and friends would cause problems, he couldn't have been prepared for the extent of the damage: within two years, Carter's marriage was over, his friends were gone, and he was fired from his job as a public school teacher, all because he was honest about his disbelief.

During the first two years of his blog, he didn't write much about his personal life, but by the time I found it he had a section titled "To My Daughters," which includes "a handful of letters to my four beautiful daughters for them to read when they are ready."

He explains to readers why he shares such personal thoughts: "I know there are many others who wrestle with how to speak to their loved ones about their skepticism. . . . Maybe in these letters some will find a helpful suggestion or two which can help move discussion in a positive direction."

I'm especially interested in the relationships he maintains by remaining in Jackson to be near his daughters, who, along with his ex-wife, siblings, and parents, attend the same church he was raised in. I decided to give him a call.

Between the time zone difference and Carter's schedule—he's teaching in a new school with several side jobs and lots of running around for errands and family commitments—it took a few tries for us to connect via video chat. When we finally settled in for a long conversation one Sunday night, he, frankly, looked a little tired. In his forties now, with light brown hair, a focused manner, and slightly shy smile, he's living in Jackson with his partner of several years and her son from a previous marriage. Two nights a week after work, he goes to the house he used to live in to be with his daughters, cooking dinner, helping with homework, and hanging out until it's time for sleep.

One of the first things I needed to straighten out when I spoke with him was how long Carter went before telling his daughters that he's not Christian; on his blog, he writes about what it's like to drive them to youth revivals, baptisms, and other church events. His answer surprised me: He kept it a secret from them for four years. His first "coming out" meant telling his wife, parents, and siblings, who, he says, were devastated. Hoping to keep their marriage intact, the couple began weekly counseling with a Baptist preacher who has a PhD in marriage and family counseling from a seminary. This was a mistake, Carter says. Approaching their sessions with the belief that a marriage cannot be healthy unless it's based on faith, their therapist had no tools to deal with an unbeliever in a relationship with a believer. He ultimately warned them that Carter's nonbelief would have an adverse effect on the children, which prompted Carter's wife to ask him to keep it a secret, even after they decided to divorce.

"She was afraid it would have a big impact on them—that if I didn't believe anymore, it would take away the credibility of their religion."

Carter acquiesced with his ex-wife's request. "It was the elephant in the living room we were all walking around," he said.

The couple agreed on joint custody, but, even after working three jobs to cover the increased expenses from the divorce, Carter couldn't afford his own place. His daughters stayed with his ex-wife in the home they had once shared.

One of those new jobs was teaching at his daughters' school so he could continue to have a daily presence in their lives. During the 2012 election, one of his history students became suspicious about Carter's political views after a lesson on the electorate numbers predicted Barack Obama would win over Mitt Romney.

"I was one of the few teachers at the school who was not telling them Romney would win. I was one of the few teachers *not* giving my opinion."

I asked Carter to clarify: We're talking about a public school, right?

"Yes, but this is Mississippi. The administration is almost all Christian. They have this belief that they are on a mission field. That their schools are battlegrounds for the souls of children, even though the children are *also* almost all Christian."

His student combed through Carter's social media accounts, looking for and finding evidence of his "liberal" views and outing him to other classmates, parents, and teachers as an atheist. After being transferred from teaching history to math soon after without an explanation, Carter ended the academic year with a letter from the superintendent saying he was "not welcome to work in any capacity at any school facility" for the rest of his life.

Carter knew that what the school had done was illegal, but he did not want to fight it because of his daughters' attendance there. Keeping his promise to his ex-wife, he would still not tell his girls, but after losing his job he decided he wouldn't hide this part of himself from the public anymore. He'd been active in an online support group for nonbelievers in Mississippi, and most were anonymous, including the seventy-year-old moderator, a neurologist who feared losing his practice if he were outed. Carter looked at these examples and knew he didn't want to keep living a secret life.

"Once you lose enough things, there's nothing left to take away," he explained to me on his decision to write using his real name. "That's where I was. There was nothing else that could be taken from me. I had lost my marriage, my house, my kids, my job, all my friends. I had nothing left. I decided I'm going to start writing and I don't care who finds out."

I asked him how his oldest daughters, teenagers by this point, could not have known about his public life online. Part of it, he believes, is the way children sense which topics are awkward for their parents, and, he says, with a family full of sensitive people, none of them seemed to want to know.

"While they are all intelligent and curious, they seemed to have turned off their curiosity about this one thing," he explained.

Carter's writing found a large audience right away, and he began getting invitations to speak at conferences and with small groups. He met his new partner though the online support group for nonbelievers, and she fully supports his work. While he can't confirm that anyone in his own family reads his writing, there is one person who does: his partner's mother, which caused another all-too-familiar problem.

When his partner's parents found out about his public life, they met with the couple and, after two years of welcoming him into their home for holidays and gatherings, they confronted Carter with a video of him at a speaking event they'd found online and forbade him to come onto their property. His partner tried to explain to her parents that she was a nonbeliever before Carter, that they had met through the online support group that she'd joined first. Carter laughs as he remembers, "Our parents ended up meeting each other and hit it off, but they each believed it was the other couple's child who'd turned theirs into an atheist."

With Carter not welcome in her parents' home, their daughter (an only child) and her son also stopped going. Not long after, his partner's father died.

"He cut her out of his will because of me," Carter said.

I asked Carter how this affects him. Had he been wrong before when he thought he'd already lost everything?

"I feel guilt about it. If I wasn't around, she'd have a better relationship with her family. But she says it's not my fault."

One night, four years after his divorce and two years after he began blogging, he embraced a chance to have the inevitable discussion with his girls. One of his younger daughters asked about a conference he was traveling for that weekend. He thought about calling it a "writers' conference," but he also had been looking for an organic way to let his daughters know more about who he is, so he was upfront: "It's a conference for people who used to be Christian and now they're not," he told her.

His daughter, whom he describes as stirring a bowl of brownie mix at the kitchen counter, "wouldn't look at me. She just kept stirring."

"So . . . you would be one of those people?" she asked him.

"Yes," he said.

She sighed. "That's what I was afraid of."

Carter decided it was time to sit down with each of the girls and tell them that he was no longer a Christian. He continues to be surprised about how little they want to know, and he doesn't often bring it up. He can tell how uncomfortable it makes them, he says.

"Right now what's more important is that they feel unguarded and comfortable with me. If I were to try to talk directly about differences between what they believe and what I believe, it would introduce a distance between us, and I can't live with that. I can't deal with that emotional distance. It's physically painful to me."

Despite everything he's been through, he's not leaving Dixie any time soon. The youngest of his daughters is nine, and they are his priority.

"I'm a strong believer in the family unit, so I'm biased toward doing whatever it takes to keep that bond strong."

In a letter to his daughters titled "The Silver Lining in Your Situation," he acknowledges that they may sometimes feel cheated out of a more harmonious family situation, that it would be simpler if their parents agreed on most things, like many of their friends' parents. "But," he writes, "I'm not convinced that means it's necessarily better. . . . On such a lifelong journey it can be a great asset that in your own family you find more than one way of looking at the world."

The letter concludes with ideas that he reiterated to me in our conversation: his hope that being in intimate relationships with people who believe different things can make us all more tolerant and accepting. He's also wary of becoming a stereotype to his family, a reason why he avoids fully offering his opinion on hot-button social issues.

"I want to be careful that they don't ever fall into stereotypical thinking about me, like 'oh, he's an atheist so he believes this and that . . .' because I'm not a stereotype and I don't want to encourage that," he told me.

"All I know to do is keep being me. Success, to me, would be to make it to the girls' adulthood helping them see that people who believe differently than them are still people they can respect."

After hearing Neil Carter's story, I think of how, in some ways, though we live in the same country, we also live in different worlds. I don't face his level of dilemma on a regular basis, risking entire relationships, a home, or a job by being sincere about who I am. But having grown up in families who value religion as a unifying factor, the essence of our issues can be boiled down quickly. While it's not a threat to my marriage or relationship with my kids, I do know what it feels like to wish I felt fully accepted by people who make up the tapestry I've been a part of from the beginning. When Carter decided, so many years ago, to unify the fractured parts of himself, he had to ask a question (albeit one with much more extreme consequences) that many of us ask ourselves, even if it's only prompted at the holidays, when our families bow their heads in prayer: How much does my need for sincerity weigh against the threat it might have to this relationship?

Having children, which often nudges us to reconnect or strengthen ties with family, can force issues into the light that might have been easier to keep hidden. It might not have been a problem, before kids, to avoid a religious service, mealtime prayer, or conversation about a controversial issue. But children have a way of whirling through our placid routines with fresh air and blowing those closet doors wide open. For those of us who decide to maintain or even encourage connection (while acknowledging that, for some, it can be too painful or challenging to do so), it may take consideration and conscious effort to make those connections as nourishing as possible.

Carter writes that he fields questions on a weekly basis from couples hoping to work out differences in belief and recommends the book *In Faith and In Doubt* by Dale McGowan, an atheist married to a Southern Baptist, who spent four years researching families who have made it work. When I look at Carter's suggestions, inspired by the book and hindsight from his own experience, I find many are applicable not only to couples but also to *any* two people willing to prioritize relationship over belief: I think of my relationship with one of my closest friends, who also happens to be a preacher's wife, and other friends from my past who feel more like family. I think of my siblings and their partners. I think of my aunts, uncles, cousins, all of those people I grew up alongside, who taught me the value of family in the first place. Like Neil Carter, I've found the need to be upfront about the fact that my beliefs are no longer what they used to be, but I also want to balance that need against prioritizing those connections.

One of the most accessible of Carter's suggestions is that we remember to focus on similarities more than differences. If we set aside labels for one another and remember that rarely does *any* one person's ideas match up perfectly with the generalizations of a group, we often find that we have more in common than not. Another suggestion is that we protect one another from disrespect. For me, this has meant staying away from conversation or reading that I might agree with but that disparages others or reinforces stereotypes. Our children, too, might hear this kind of rhetoric on television, at school, or with friends, and this is a time when their connections with various family members will help inform their understanding that we're all more complex than the labels would have us believe.

Even when we play it safe and avoid controversial discussion, emphasize our similarities, and work on tolerance, we will still run into language, ideas, or practices that can create tension out of nowhere. For Carter, this may be an invitation to his daughter's baptism. For me, it may be hearing someone say, "I'm praying for you," or being asked to bow my head for prayer. In moments like these, we can make a choice: Does what is required of me make such an impact that it should come between this relationship?

Sometimes, depending on the issue and the relationship, the answer might be yes. For the chapter on secular morality, I considered the ways family life is an ideal context in which to practice balancing our own needs against those of others. Those high levels of morality that parent-coach Chris White had me consider are not quite as simple as putting the needs of others before our own if it means forgoing our sense of dignity. White referred to this quality as being *sincere*, which he described as being anchored in our own truths with the flexibility to accommodate others. This need for sincerity strikes me as the reason for dilemmas that come up in our rooted relationships.

For me, these days, as much as I've come to value rooted relationships after moving so far away from them, the answer is no, what is required of me does not make such an impact that it should come between us. I use religious vernacular as an example, especially as it seems to be a source of irritation for nonbelievers. Phrases like "God bless you," "You're in my prayers," or "God has a plan" can hit up against an invisible wall surrounding a nonbeliever, with the person who says it being none the wiser. But rather than dismissing this language (and letting it divide us), I've been working to maintain connection by translating it into something more universal. "I'm praying for you" becomes *I'm thinking of you.* "It's in God's hands" becomes *It is what it is.* "It's part of a bigger plan" becomes *I'm hoping for the best.*

It's compromises like this that people on both sides of the religious divide have a problem with, and I understand why. We all have reasons, based on experience and development, that add weight in the balance between our need for sincerity and our need to be part of a group. But as we continue creating those family narratives, it's helpful to remember that the most effective explore the ups *and* downs; the sincerest version I can offer my children might be the one that integrates who I am now with the occasional reminder that *this is where I'm from.*

SEVEN KEYS TO MAKING A MIXED-BELIEF RELATIONSHIP WORK

This is by Dale McGowan, author of *In Faith and In Doubt: How Religious Believers and Nonbelievers Can Create Strong Marriages and Loving Families.*

1. *Never try to convert or deconvert the other person.* In matters of belief, support and encourage his or her autonomy. If they begin to question their own opinions and want a sounding board, they know where to find you.
2. *Focus on shared values more than different beliefs.* While the difference in beliefs is there, people can choose where to place their focus and emphasis. Values (opinions about what is good) impact daily life more than most beliefs (opinions about what is true), and values tend to overlap more often than specific beliefs.
3. *Make personal respect nonnegotiable, even if you question and challenge each other's ideas.* Ideas and opinions must earn respect. However, respect for each other as people is a nonnegotiable requirement of any relationship.
4. *Engage in and learn about each other's worldviews.* Make the effort to learn more about the other person's religious belief or nonbelief conviction. It's a gesture of personal respect and a great way to get to know each other.
5. *Remember that the opinions of believers are not always the same as the doctrines of their churches, and the opinions of nonbelievers are not al-*

ways the same as those of prominent atheists. Take the time to find out whether and how the other person's beliefs differ from the stereotype.

6. *Support and protect each other from mistreatment.* If your friend, relative, or partner is being maligned, pressured, or ostracized because of his or her beliefs, especially by family or community members who share your worldview, you are in a unique position to come to his or her defense. Never miss an opportunity to do so.

7. *Spread the word!* As moderating voices with real-world experiences, people in mixed-belief relationships of all kinds have the power to dispel negative stereotypes. When churchgoers start suggesting that all atheists are immoral, or when the local atheist group starts suggesting that all religious people are unintelligent, you know better. Find the courage to speak up.

8

HOLIDAYS, TRADITIONS, AND RITUALS

Everything is ceremony in the wild garden of childhood.

—Pablo Neruda

I don't remember how Chris and I ended up with six-month-old twins dressed as vegetables—a chili pepper and a pea pod, to be precise—the first Halloween we were parents. I want to say the costumes were gifts, but I'll admit the whole thing sounds very much like the result of a middle-of-the-night-nursing/Internet-browsing session. Regardless, they were pretty cute, as far as produce goes, and we wanted to show them off. At the last minute, we decided to throw on overalls (an article of clothing every good Kansan should own), dress as farmers, and take the veggies downtown, where we'd heard there was annual storefront trick-or-treating.

We did not head out the door that night intending for Halloween to become our family thing. The twins were just babies, doing what babies do, clueless to the fact that they were bundled edibles, but Chris and I were ignited by the All Hallows spark. In our Midwestern college town, we discovered, students ranging in age from preschool to graduate school flock downtown to the local businesses, which open their doors after hours and offer candy from cauldrons and wheelbarrows. Some turn their stores and aisles into haunted houses and mazes. Everyone dresses up: kids, parents, professors, managers, staff. The restaurants overflow with happy witches and silly superheroes, nibbling candy, drinking beer, eating French fries. Neither of us had participated in the festivities before becoming parents but realized, at least in this town, you're never too old to be something for Halloween.

For the next five years, the downtown trick-or-treat tour was tradition, and our family's passion for Halloween blossomed. While the twins were young, we dressed in themes: the farmers and veggies, Dr. Seuss characters, a family of pirates. Within a few years, though, the boys were ready to fulfill their own costume visions and left Chris and I on our own to coordinate. With Thanksgivings and Christmases in flux as we rotated between extended families, Halloween became our immediate family's most consistent annual tradition, the holiday we made our own. The summer we moved to California, I had a harder time thinking of being away for Halloween more than any other day. And then, our first October on the West Coast, I got a package in the mail.

It was from a family friend who knew about our love for the holiday and encouraged us to keep it going in our new home, but this prop was a different take for me: I was looking at an impressively sized, grisly skeleton in a purple torn robe meant to hang midair, complete with flashing eye sockets and groaning noises. It was the kind of decoration one might read about in the editorial section of the paper, written by concerned neighborhood parents with scared children.

I pulled it out of the box, and the child in me thought, *Uh . . . this is not allowed.* Over the years, I'd unconsciously gravitated toward a "nice" version of Halloween, limiting décor to gourds and pumpkins and keeping our costumes sweet. I remember being morbidly intrigued by the scary stuff when I was young, the witches, ghosts, and goblins, but I was taught that this holiday was about celebrating evil and exists for bad people who want to do bad things. If it were only up to my dad, we wouldn't have participated at all, but my sister and I begged to dress up for school parties and my mom put costumes together for us, with guidelines: no black, no blood, no gore, no guts. We went as cheerleaders, princesses, brides. My sister and I sometimes did a small amount of trick-or-treating in the neighborhood, but usually we attended religious autumn festivals, where we bobbed for apples, drank hot cider, and maybe went on a hay bale ride. The candy was the thing, though. We always, one way or another, got loads of candy.

Like most kids, my younger sister and I cherished our loot and developed intricate rituals around it, involving inventory, division, and trade. We hid it under our beds from imagined trespassers and set limits on to how much we'd eat in a day, both wanting to be the last one to still have a supply by Christmas. We organized the candy and reorganized the candy and filed it away in ranking order, a complete plan for consumption.

Even though it was an ambivalent celebration, these memories of Halloween from my childhood are pleasant enough and don't include things like the skeleton I was holding. Were we missing something by not embracing the spooky side of the holiday, keeping things tame with agreeable costumes and pumpkin carving? I didn't think so.

I looked at the skeleton, which was larger than my kids, had a shiver, and thought of the sender, who doesn't have children. *He knows our youngest is three, right? There's no way I'm putting this up.* I shoved our new roommate in the hall closet before waking my daughter from her nap and picking up my first-graders from school. I'd deal with him later.

Later came quickly, however, when that same day kicked off our rainy season and one of the boys went looking for his mud boots.

"Whoa! What is this?!?!" he cried in delight, pulling the skeleton from the closet.

"Put that back, before your sister sees it! It'll scare her!" I whispered.

"It's not scary; it's funny!" he said. "You guys, come look!"

Before I could reach the closet, the others had run to see.

"A bone man!" the three-year-old laughed.

"Can we play with it?"

"Let's hang it in the front door!"

As they typically do, my children surprised me that day with their freshness, their openness, their lack of judgment. In a moment I realized *I* was terrified of an object that they viewed as a toy. Since survey course discussions on nature versus nurture, I'd been convincing myself that I could detect social conditioning from a mile away, but here I was, projecting my experience, my fears, onto my daughter, who oscillated between shrieking with laughter at the skeleton and rocking it like a baby.

"You guys *like* this thing?" I asked.

"Yes!" they cried. "Can we *please* put it up?"

I stared him down through the eye sockets.

"Okay," I said, with a perspective shift that set my imagination loose. "And let's get some tombstones to go with it."

That fall, the skeleton with the blinking eyes hung outside the front door, challenging me like my own personal Zen koan every time I passed. The kids continued to love him; they twirled him around all month and stored him with their toys for the rest of the year. But I was unsettled by his presence. Not *just* because a groaning skeleton is generally unsettling, mind you; it was more than that. There were layers of paradox contained in his ribs and questions that popped out and beckoned when I walked by, as if, assuming I followed the train of thought they set into motion, I could arrive at some greater understanding.

For one thing, I wondered about his allure. We were all drawn to him; we all wanted him on display—even me, the décor-magazine junkie who aspires to create a calm, peaceful, aesthetically pleasing home. Why? He was blatantly, unabashedly grotesque. Was this some form of rebellion? Was I experimenting with what was forbidden in my own childhood? Were my kids embracing or even conquering their fears? Did it have something to do with empowerment or liberation? I started looking into the history behind Halloween and the various reasons and ways people celebrate it—the first time I'd really thought through the layers of meaning behind a holiday symbol like this.

For another thing, facing such an ominous embodiment of our favorite holiday pushed me to be more conscious and reflective about intention. It was like we were saying, "If we're gonna do this, let's *do this*." We'd begun our Halloween tradition haphazardly, out of convenience more than anything, as the logistics—who, what, when, where, how—were already answered for us. We didn't really need to think about it; we just showed up to a party that had already been started. But after moving to a new town, with no family or traditions in place, it would take more effort on my part to see this holiday through. If only for myself, I needed to be able to answer the *why*. Why this holiday? Why any holiday? What kind of meaning do we find in them? Are there others we want to celebrate? Are there some we want to skip? How do we decide?

Finally, even though the previous five years had brought me a husband, kids, and a mortgage, it was these questions, of all things, that made me face a fact I'd been suspecting for a long time but was hesitant to embrace: I was a grown-up now. I was a decider. This first Halloween on our own preceded what would be the first Thanksgiving and Christmas and New Year's and all the other mainstream cultural holidays our kids had memorized and anticipated in chronological order by month. Chris and I were the adults they counted on to hang the decorations, coordinate the gatherings, and prepare the feasts. This skeleton reminded me that much of my kids' experience with holidays, celebrations, and traditions would depend on their parents, and I have laughably little experience in this department, as demonstrated by the fact that a ridiculous Halloween prop, mostly likely sent to us as a gag, was spinning me into a full-blown, overanalyzed, existential crisis.

I suppose I have holiday baggage. While the contemporary definition for *holiday* is "a day off"—for rest, observance, or celebration—the Old English origin is *hāligdæg*, which translates to "holy day" and was originally reserved for the religious. Typically, religions are rich with holiday traditions, and many holiday traditions are rich with religion. But the more fundamental churches I grew up in taught that the secular and commercial influence on "holy days" corrupted them entirely and rendered them unfit for observance by true believers.

Some secular families distance themselves from holidays because they're too religious; we were a religious family that distanced ourselves from holidays because they were too secular. Between the religious doctrine and our many relocations, holiday memories from my childhood are haphazard and irregular. They mainly include me wishing we could just do what everyone else was doing and my mother trying her best to make things work: the secret Halloween costumes we wore to school, unwrapped toys on Christmas morning in a bare living room, pastel dresses and hats for an Easter sunrise service.

This was my experience until adolescence, when a breakthrough in holiday tradition came at just the right time. The house we moved into when I was thirteen was a large Victorian on the wrong side of the tracks but big enough to host my mom's side of the family, who had always gathered for Christmas. With visitors coming, my mom got us our first tree—a small one, measuring three feet tall—and set it on a table in front of the bay windows. Having that tree meant so much to me that, to this day, whenever I drive past a field or open space, I search for the smallest baby evergreen and imagine it covered in lights and tinsel.

With varying religious and financial constraints limiting the way we celebrated as a group, my mom's family got creative. Simply being together meant most to us, and we loved to laugh. On Christmas Eve, after a potluck meal of soup and sandwiches and some willy-nilly neighborhood caroling, we held a talent show that went late into the night, sometimes until two or three in the morning. The younger kids took it very seriously, showcasing their singing or instrumental skills or perhaps performing a martial arts routine or magic trick. The teenagers and college students turned it into a chance for sketch comedy performances, my favorite being my older brothers' recurring "Wild Nights Away from Home." The adults played guitar and sang songs from the 1960s and performed their own skits, gently mocking their children's antics or parodying getting older. We knew we could count on the same people to fulfill certain roles: The oldest of the cousins was *always* MC. One of my mom's younger sisters *always* transformed herself into grumpy Nikolas, Santa's alter ego, with a gray mustache, scraggly Santa hat, and mysterious Eastern European accent. Grandma Jean *always* dressed as Maxine from the greeting cards, irreverent and sassy, complete with aviator sunglasses and periwinkle shower poufs poking out under a hat.

I credit those few days each winter with my mother's family for getting me through high school. They taught me that holidays aren't about doing what everyone else is doing, after all. They taught me to embrace quirks and differences. They taught me that I was part of a fun, loving, creative group, no matter how I felt at school. But just as quickly as I came to cherish this tradition, it began to get away from me. My parents separated after I graduated, which ended the gatherings in our home. My relatives worked hard to keep it going, with new people hosting and the cousins introducing boyfriends and girlfriends who would eventually become husbands and wives with families of their own. We adapted by planning to gather every other year, which proved to be difficult as well, as those families began to spread out across the country. Three years out of high school, I spent my first Christmas away from the Midwest when I took a job as a flight attendant, hunkered down in a hotel room in New Jersey with Chinese take-out and loneliness. Until I met Chris and joined his family for the holidays, I went back to my childhood ways of floundering during the season with nowhere to land.

Not only do I have little to offer my kids in the way of lasting holiday traditions from my own childhood, but I'm also not one for *any* type of routine, whether it's annual, seasonal, or otherwise. I don't know if it's the result of nature or experience or a combination of the two, but, left to my own devices, I'm not easily a creature of habit. I once had a roommate in college detail her mornings. She had my complete attention as she described the order of things: first coffee, then shower, clothes, breakfast (always toast and fruit), brush teeth, and go. Until that moment, it had never occurred to me that a person could go to bed the night before knowing exactly what the first hour of her next day would bring. No wonder she was always so calm.

"Well, how do you do it?" she asked when she noticed how captivated I was by these details.

"I don't know. . . . I sort of wake up, like, surprised, and wonder WHAT IS GOING TO HAPPEN RIGHT NOW?!?!?!"

I understand how the predictability of routine can decrease anxiety and stress, but I also like to be ready for change. I live for flexibility, thrive on spontaneity, love to watch the way life unexpectedly unfolds. I often find that my most precious moments with others occur without much planning involved. I can typically predict where a new friendship might be headed when someone says to me, "Let's get something on the calendar." It's difficult for me to make decisions and commitments about the future, which means I'm hesitant to stick to *any* routine, let alone those occurring annually.

Of course, having kids—especially starting with two at once—who seek out and thrive on routine has forced me to make adjustments. I remember getting a calendar when the twins started preschool, packed full with a schedule, holidays, and observances, some I'd never heard of, and thinking, *What's up with all this planning?* I had a vague sense that somehow we'd been trapped; apparently, what some people find comforting others interpret as restrictive. It was August, and the classroom was decked out in yellow: sunshine, sunflowers, sunglasses everywhere. As the year went on, the setting abruptly and dramatically transformed to reflect the passing of time: yellow turned orange turned red turned green; suns turned leaves turned snow turned flowers. The changes were reflected in the songs they sang, the games they played, the food they ate, the holidays they celebrated. Their days revolved around concrete, embodied experiences of time and change.

Those early school days gave me a much better understanding of the way children depend on routine and ritual to manage and measure time, to find both comfort and delight in its passing. Kids can memorize the days of the week and the months in a year, but these are just abstract concepts compared to marking time and change in a way they can see, hear, smell, taste, and touch. Since research began in the 1950s, psychologists have found that meaningful ritual in a child's life, whether it's during a holiday, rite of passage, or weeknight meal, benefits our children in a number of ways, including academically, emotionally, and socially.

The difference between routine and ritual is small but crucial. Both "routine" and "ritual" describe actions that are performed in a regular, prescribed order, but what sets ritual apart is something we can't see: the attitude, meaning, and intent behind the actions. Routine focuses on *completing* the tasks while ritual focuses on *performing* the tasks. We tend to associate ritual with religious practice, but any routine can become a meaningful ritual based on the purpose and symbolism we prescribe it. Writer Maria Popova describes routine and ritual as two sides of the same coin: "While routine aims to make the chaos of everyday life more containable and controllable, ritual aims to imbue the mundane with an element of the magical."[1]

Children seem able to elevate almost any experience with deeper meaning, as I remember doing with a precious ritual from the summers of my childhood: the drive to Bible camp. To the adult chaperones, it might have just been an annual task, getting a caravan of kids from point A (church) to point B (church camp). But in my mind, a drive lasting only a few hours through southwest Missouri stretches beyond the confines of time and geography, where the car I'm in, the people I'm with, the music we listen to, the gas stations we stop at, and the snacks we eat sparkle and float in my memory, as if the whole voyage is covered in pixie dust. This drive took place once a year, for eight years, and I'll never forget how hard I sobbed in the backseat on the way home from my last summer as a camper when I realized this routine, so heavy with symbolism—of innocence, trust, identity, belonging, acceptance—was coming to an end.

As intention, then, transforms routine into ritual, time and other people transform ritual into tradition. The Latin root words for *tradition* are *trans*, which means "across," and *dare*, which means "to give": "to give across." The two words, when combined as *tradare*, means "to deliver" or "to hand down." Traditions serve as connectors, linking one year, generation, or person to the next. Traditions tell a story about identity; they're a group's way of saying, "This is who we are and this is what we value." Even my own experience of *not* having much in the way of tradition is its own kind of tradition; it tells its own kind of story.

By definition, tradition is about establishing and nurturing connection across time and people, which benefits our children in a number of ways. A predictable set of behaviors and activities offers children stability and security. Opportunities for everyone to feel that they contribute helps our kids shape identity and a sense of purpose. Making room for everyone involved, regardless of differences in age and lifestyle, combats self-centeredness and encourages empathy and generosity. When I look at the lists of benefits that tradition offers us, I notice they are many of the same things religion can provide. It seems important, then, for families who aren't religious to find meaningful traditions of their own.

I understand, however, that this is easier said than done. Establishing meaningful rituals and traditions is a dilemma parents refer to often when we discuss raising kids outside of religion. For as much as tradition has to offer, it also presents challenges: it doesn't always allow for change and growth; it limits the possibility for new experiences and adventures; it can offer us a false sense of security or cause us to become complacent. We may grasp at traditions from our pasts, even though they feel hollow or insincere; we might experiment with borrowed rituals from other cultures or groups that feel silly or coerced; we may give up, dismissing the significance of ritual and tradition, and watch seasons turn and years go by with nothing but a vague sense of unease and restlessness from the disconnection we experience when we aren't sure what, exactly, "to give across."

As I discovered when we moved, it's both liberating and daunting to be free from constraints that inform our rituals and traditions. I find that considering tradition outside of religion has the same type of advantages and challenges that we faced after moving away from family, friends, and a familiar community. On the one hand, the possibilities are endless. We can determine for ourselves what values we want to express, what connections we want to nurture, when, where, and how we do it, and make the necessary adjustments. On the other hand, precisely *because* the possibilities are endless and we *can* make adjustments, we may notice "tradition" lacking in qualities that help define it: predictability, commitment, endurance.

It's difficult to feel committed to something when we aren't certain why we're doing it in the first place, which is why understanding what our children gain from various traditions can inform the way we establish them. It helps that traditions are available in a variety of ways and serve so many purposes. A big, classic, holiday gathering with extended family is going to meet different needs than an intimate, eclectic, weekly ritual at home. When trying to work through it all, I find the "Holiday Season" a good place to start. Because this annual time frame, which covers the postautumnal equinox to postwinter solstice, is so rife with observances, celebrations, and cultural traditions, it's not hard to take a closer look and come up with intentions, ideas, and perspectives that inject a personal touch within a framework already in place.

Strip away the commercial influence, historical myth, and religious veneer, and the string of holidays from October to January ultimately brings moments for observation, reflection, gratitude, and connection during a season when we need it most. For a long time, I considered these holidays mere distractions from the fact that the days were getting shorter, the nights colder, the earth more brittle and dry—as if we were trying to deny reality with sugar and twinkle lights. But beginning with a closer look into Halloween, the first holiday to kick off the darkening days leading to a winter climax, I realized how much more each holiday means when, instead of being a distraction or attempt to make the season what we want it to be, we use it to acknowledge and focus on what is.

As my children encourage me to embrace the menacing side of Halloween, I've realized that we're celebrating a subversion of expectations: if only for a day, irreverence, taboo, and defiance are the norm, something our whole family enjoys. It's a celebration of creativity and imagination, too. Without many restrictions on their costumes, the kids gravitate toward the disturbing, like the "blood princess" my six-year-old conceived of on her own. Even though we've settled in a rural area with few neighbors to bother, we still put out the hanging skeleton and tombstones; over the years, we've added spider webs, purple lights, and a bloody, stumpy appendage. I see my children facing and embracing what they might fear and, as a result, being less afraid. They've taught me to do it, too. For them, it's ghosts and goblins; for me, it's the dark days ahead.

Sometimes us nonbelievers are suspicious of putting too much into holidays that the religious claim as their own, but it helps to remember that secular seasonal celebrations have been around longer than the updated religious versions. Within the context of a year, the darker aspects of Halloween represent one part of a natural, universal cycle of death and rebirth, which is ultimately what we find ourselves celebrating around the end of December.

I've found that focusing on the changes in the natural world and determining what values we express when we celebrate can help make the more popular holidays feel personally resonant, which in turn encourages commitment. The Christmases I spent with my maternal extended family remind me that we can work around the need for flexibility by being inventive. The limiting factor we currently face during Christmas each year is that we rotate locations. We've worked around the need for flexibility in location by making it our one consistent family tradition to attend the *Nutcracker* ballet, which we've seen now in five different cities. The first time we saw it (on a whim, as is typical for us), when the boys were toddlers and my daughter was not yet born, we were overcome by a combination of the fantastical magic and beauty of the performance, recognition of the familiar music, and formal setting of the theater. Establishing this as tradition was the right fit for us, and now it's the one ritual at Christmas my kids can count on, no matter where we are and who else might be with us.

It helps, too, knowing that, as long as we provide some regularity, our children are perfectly capable of grabbing onto what means most to them. They will notice the smallest detail in a routine and determine its significance without our input. I think of what stands out to my children most about our Thanksgivings on the West Coast. For the longest time, the prospect of planning and preparing a Thanksgiving meal on my own was the last thing I wanted to do. But I also wanted to gather for Thanksgiving in California with my siblings, who, like me, do not hold tightly onto classic traditions.

The first time we drove to Southern California for the holiday, Chris and I offered to bring the turkey and prepare the meal. It was the first time we'd ever cooked a turkey, and Chris, after doing some research, decided he wanted to brine it for two days before our six-hour drive south. After working through some logistical challenges, we ended up transporting the bird in a bright orange plastic bucket from a hardware store containing an ice-water brine. This traveling orange turkey bucket became symbolic to our children. Because us adults have trouble committing, for the past five years we've wondered out loud what we might do for Thanksgiving, and our children look at us as though we've lost our minds.

"We're going to see the cousins with a turkey in the bucket," they say. "It's tradition."

We can learn from the fresh perspective of children. Adults might think of traditions as needing to be ancient and stodgy to have brevity. They do not. Traditions that stand the test of time aren't meaningful because they're old; they're old because they're meaningful. Incidentally, after I realized how fulfilling it is to spend an entire day preparing a meal with no other stress or distractions, the process itself, the celebration, Thanksgiving has become one of my favorite holidays. The point of the flawed historical narrative around Thanksgiving is that we celebrate differences and connections by contributing to the meal however we can. It's a great day to express gratitude for our connections, in whatever form they take: we have friends who aren't able to join family at Thanksgiving and share a "Friendsgiving" with another family in the same position.

Outside of standard American holidays, I've found it helpful to consider lesser-known religious or cultural practices to inform rituals we can make our own. Several years ago I mentioned to a friend, who is a member of the Nazarene Church, that I suffer from major postholiday blues around the New Year. She pointed out that in the Christian liturgical calendar, the "Twelve Days of Christmas" is more than just a confusing song about birds and instruments. These twelve days, between Christmas Eve and Christian Epiphany, are a time for celebration and feasting, which ends on the Twelfth Night. I looked into customs for the Twelfth Night and found that pre-Christian Europe celebrated it as the end of the "Lord of Misrule," the time of upheaval beginning on Halloween that symbolizes the world being turned upside down. I was delighted to find that a Twelfth Night celebration bridges the gap between the winter solstice and early new year *and* brings our family's passion for Halloween full circle. This inspired me to create a new custom for our family: a Twelfth Night celebration, when we take down the Christmas decorations and have a chaotic dinner where kids are in charge and grown-ups misbehave: a mark of closure to the season of misrule.

The author of *Religion for Atheists* and School of Life cofounder Alain de Botton would call what I'm doing "reverse colonization," a practice he encourages nonbelievers to consider as we learn from what makes religious rituals meaningful. In an interview with Krista Tippett for the podcast *On Being*, de Botton explains, "In the same way that Christianity colonized the pagan world, absorbing its best elements," he says, "so I'm arguing that nonbelievers today can do a little bit of this with religion just as religion did it with them."[2]

Without realizing what we were doing, a few years ago Chris and I pulled another reverse colonization on the ritual of saying grace before a meal. It started when we realized during a holiday with family that our kids had no idea what to do during a prayer. We don't expect them to pray (or pretend to), but we do want them to understand that it's a time they need to be silent and still. We also appreciate that the ritual of grace encourages us to be reflective about gratitude, so we started our own version, saying "thankfuls" before any meal we sit down to share together. As a family, we don't voice thankfuls to an invisible being but to one another. Establishing this as a ritual means it's not optional: no one can shrug it off because of a bad mood; it serves as a touchstone for us to measure hectic days against; it's a practice for all of us to reflect on gratitude and listen to one another with respect.

As we progress, shaping rituals for our immediate families that express our values and offer our children a sense of stability, identity, and contribution, one more thing we consider about tradition within larger groups—extended family, friends, and community—is that they are a way to connect with others. This means that the ritual itself may not personally resonate with us, which is not so much the point as the connections it nurtures. Our children benefit from these types of tradition, too, by understanding their place in a larger context. Being around people who are older or younger than them, or who have different ideas, needs, and desires, encourages selflessness, empathy, and understanding and further shapes their sense of identity and belonging.

The Christmases I've spent with my husband's family have been valuable lessons in what it means "to give across." I spent my first holiday with this group, whose plans are so grounded in routine that they move like a unit, asking, "What's happening now?" But over time, I learned how tradition can turn "they" into "we." And there's one tradition I now share with them that I was surprised to find made me uneasy: the whole Santa thing. When the boys were very young, the ritual seemed innocent enough: the children leave a letter, cookies, and carrots by the fireplace and hang stockings on the mantel. After sharing hot chocolate over a reading of *'Twas the Night before Christmas*, they go to bed and the grown-ups fill the stockings, nibble the treats, and leave presents behind for the morning. It's the very tradition I had dreamed about as a child.

But as the twins got older and began to ask more sophisticated and critical questions, I began to more seriously consider why I was—let's be real here—*lying* to them and got very uneasy when Santa came up. Essentially, I was learning about how it all worked at the same time they were. When they asked me questions, I'd direct them to Chris or ask him myself, out of their earshot: How *does* Santa make it to all these houses in one night? What *does* happen if a house doesn't have a chimney? Why *was* he in two spots in the same day, at the mall and in front of the grocery store?

The more elaborate and duplicitous the Santa myth became, and the more coaching I needed just to perpetuate it, the less I wanted to be involved. I presented my dilemma to Chris, who defends this tradition with passion based on his own ethereal, positive experience as a child. That this tradition connects his experience with our children's outweighs my discomfort over it, and we've landed in a place shaped by trial and error, with me being honest, yet opaque, with the kids. When they ask me questions, I tell them that I didn't know Santa as a child, that not everyone does, that they'll need to ask their dad or relatives about the details, which at least solves one problem for me, perhaps my most pressing concern: the importance of understanding that not everyone shares the same beliefs and experiences.

The Santa issue is a point of contention for many of the nonreligious, just as it is for the religious. Chris's line of thinking around the issue is similar to secular parent Dale McGowan's argument for Santa: McGowan, author of *Parenting beyond Belief* and *Raising Freethinkers*, claims that secular holiday myths are some of the first practice for our children to think critically, question authority, and come to their own conclusions, skills that will shape their lives.[3]

In addition to regularly occurring traditions, there's another category of ritual I find lacking in life outside religion: the rite of passage. These rituals, which signify and celebrate the transition from one life stage to the next, are abundant for children in religious communities: circumcision, christening, baptism, bar and bat mitzvah, and confirmation are all rites of passage, centering a child's identity around the church. The coming-of-age rite of passage, marking the transition from childhood to adulthood, is an especially crucial time to reinforce the connection between an individual and the group, encourage reflection about values and identity, and honor a child's life in a way that embraces the inevitability of change.

The rite of passage is not meant to suggest that transformation is accomplished in the space of one ceremony (baby showers do not a mother make), but it does offer the comforts of recognition and support for our children in what can be overwhelming and confusing times of change. While the nonreligious community doesn't have standard models for these rituals, a basic understanding of what they are and why they're important can help us shape our own.

In the landmark 1909 book *The Rites of Passage*, ethnographer Arnold van Gennep identified three stages a rite of passage consists of: separation, transition, and incorporation.[4] If we think of "passage" as moving from one group to another, then a withdrawal, or separation, from the current way of life is required as the person prepares for the change. The stage of transition marks a time of ambiguity, when the person has left one group but does not yet belong to another. Finally, the last stage, incorporation, is the one most Western rites of passage emphasize, which is a celebration of the person's new status.

During these times of transition, our children are particularly thirsty for rituals filled with meaning, symbolism, and brevity. If we don't provide a way to fill this need, they construct their own. While we don't have to turn to religion as a default, we also don't want to dismiss the importance of marking and celebrating transition. Just as traditions celebrating the same holiday vary widely, there is not a one-size-fits-all approach to a rite of passage. Reflecting on what values we want to emphasize, the community we want to create, and how we might foster our children's sense of belonging and worth is a good place to start when shaping rituals our children can carry with them through times of transition.

A ritual we've established since moving near the coast is our (often impulsive) stops at the beach after school on free afternoons. One of my favorite things about watching waves come in from the ocean is the way they are simultaneously predictable and surprising. When we hit the sand, my children run to the water's edge and do the same thing I did when I was younger: balance along the line created where the last wave hit the shore.

They study the spot, knowing another one is coming but not sure exactly how it will hit and where it will begin to recede. Sometimes the next one comes up short and I can sense their disappointment as they chase after it. Sometimes the rushing water surprises them and washes over their feet and legs, leaving them laughing and scrambling for higher ground.

The traditions we cultivate work like the tide to the shore, guaranteeing some sense of rhythm and predictability. But the way the water breaks and where it hits is always a bit of a mystery. Sometimes it falls short, leaving us grasping and disappointed. Sometimes it overwhelms with abundance, leaving us ecstatic and fulfilled. At times, our children will run toward them, and, at other times, they will back away. As we work "to give across," they balance on the shore, ready with anticipation and willing, when needed, to adjust.

WHY FAMILY TRADITIONS AND RITUALS ARE IMPORTANT FOR CHILDREN

Rebecca Fraser-Thill, a teacher of developmental psychology, offers this list of research-based benefits that tradition has for kids. Understanding the impact tradition has on children helps inform the ones we establish and participate in.

"Although enacting family traditions, rites, and rituals can take a good deal of planning on the part of the adults in the family," she writes, "the developmental benefits these practices provide to children and teens make the effort well worth it." Here are the top five:

1. *A Sense of Belonging*: Family traditions, rites, and rituals act as a form of symbolic communication that lets everyone involved know "this is who we are." Through the practices, family beliefs and values can be passed across generations. Children and teens can look to these recurring moments to gain knowledge of the group they belong to and what the group stands for.

   Notably, group cohesiveness increases and family relationships improve through regular enacting of traditions and rituals. Children and teens in particular feel more secure knowing that they belong to a group that has depth, continuity, and a unique culture.

2. *Personal Identity*: Recurring, meaningful family practices not only allow the group to identify with one another but also help individuals in the family gain a sense of their personal identity. This is particularly true for adolescents, who are in a developmental stage that is intensely focused on identity development.

   Research has shown that children and teens who regularly experience family traditions, rituals, and routines have a more cohesive sense of who they are compared to children and teens who do not experience these family practices. Young members of families with these practices have higher levels of lovability, which is a sense of being worthy of love, being accepted as an individual, and being aware that they can count on others.

3. *Stability, Even During Tough Times*: Family traditions and rituals provide a sense of mooring and stability. They are something individuals can look forward to and count on, which is particularly important when life feels chaotic. In any child or teenager's life, a certain degree of uncertainty inevitably exists due to the sheer quantity of social, emotional, intellectual, and physical changes happening within and around them. For children who are experiencing illness, death, and/or divorce in the family, the sense of chaos can be compounded and overwhelming.

   Rituals help head off discomfort and confusion by allowing the family to have a shared moment of relief, recentering their focus on an event that is unchanged and "normative." This normative sense is based both on comparisons with other families ("we're like everyone else") and on comparisons with the past ("even though things have shifted, we are still doing things the way we used to").

4. *A Feeling of Being Useful and Needed*: Children and teens can gain a sense of their own abilities and their role within the family through ways they contribute. From the youngest child who draws rudimentary place cards for the dinner table to the college-age individual who prepares a main dish, every dependent member of the family can be involved in recurring family practices. Enabling children to feel useful and needed is vital to their sense of self-worth, agency, and positive development.

5. *Lasting Positive Emotions*: Given the previous points, it's not surprising that recurring, meaningful family practices can improve children

and teens' emotional state. Traditions, rites, and rituals can impact all family members by providing a designated time and space for the giving and receiving of emotional support and care. In addition, rituals can be remembered for months and years to come, providing the positive emotional experience all over again with each mental replay, even after family members have passed away. Indeed, it is often these recurring moments that children and teens first think of and reminisce about after a loved one has died, providing a sense of comfort after loss that society has traditionally turned to religion to provide.

WAYS TO EMBRACE TRADITION

- Lighten up! Traditions don't have to be serious and stodgy to be meaningful. Take a look at some of the activities your family has already established as routine and ask your children what parts they enjoy and why. Consider what the activity expresses about the group and how each person can participate. With intention and commitment, these become your family's traditions.
- Own it. Reflect on your values and the things that give your family life meaning so that you are fully behind the actions. Consider the historical and/or philosophical reasons and meanings behind established traditions and create versions of your own to honor those that resonate. If you notice something lacking—an activity that expresses generosity or service, for example—come up with an activity that reflects this value and fold it in.
- Make room for others. Traditions are connectors; they link us to one another, which requires patience, understanding, and compromise. Remember, just as we don't always resonate with traditions from past generations, so our children won't always resonate with ours. Participating in tradition can be a practice in selflessness and acceptance.
- Allow for flexibility. While a defining component of tradition is its predictability, we also must allow for (and even embrace) change and differences. The level of flexibility needed won't be the same for every family. Perhaps the location is always different, but the activity is the same. Or the location is the same, but some of the people participating

rotate. Families who struggle with differences in worldview or belief can still come together to celebrate shared values in creative ways that work for everyone.

- Be committed. Because tradition can serve as a touchstone in times of change and difficulty, it's important to keep it going even when the going gets rough. It can sometimes feel like pressure or burden on the leaders of the group, but if you're struggling, take a moment to reflect on the benefits, talk to your kids about what they find meaningful, and make adjustments that work for the entire family.

OPPORTUNITIES TO ESTABLISH TRADITION

- *Weekly*: Using input from everyone involved, set a nonnegotiable block of time aside each week for the family to participate in an activity together that expresses your values. Rituals can center around food (in both preparation and consumption), an activity in nature (a hike, bike ride, or time in the park), participation in the arts (a museum, concert, or theater), or anything that reflects the story of your family: a sporting event, game night, a group trip to the library. Ritual and tradition is not so much *what* you do; it's *how* you do it, together: with regularity, intention, and commitment.

- *Seasonal*: Consider the natural changes around you and find sensory ways to capture and reflect those changes. Make sure everyone has a job: hang lights during the winter months, plant a garden during spring, take a late-night solstice walk in the summer, prepare warm and comforting foods for the first day of fall.

- *Annual*: Traditions and rituals stick the way they do because they recognize and fill universal human needs. Be curious about the history and purpose behind any tradition, religious or secular, and settle on the ones that most resonate with your family. Don't be afraid to repurpose and reclaim a tradition to make it more meaningful. Those traditions that personally resonate are the ones that stick.

CONCLUSION

On Needing Community

Never doubt that a small group of thoughtful, committed citizens can change the world. Indeed, it is the only thing that ever has.

—Margaret Mead

Those first several weeks after Chris and I became parents, the distinction between nights and days excruciatingly fuzzy, neighbors, friends, and family brought warm, nourishing foods to our home. We were so incredibly grateful for this most practical of customs. More than a decade later, I still remember who brought what and how it smelled, looked, and tasted. There's one delivery that stands out most, though, because it showed up in the hands of a complete stranger: someone from the church Grandma Jean attended had heard our news and dropped off a casserole on behalf of the congregation.

This gesture meant so much to me and also made me very sad. Not even a month into the parenting gig, and I was confronted with how different our life as a young family would be compared to the one I knew growing up. Church casseroles had been a huge part of my childhood; they represent a kind of compassion that honors our most primal needs and expects nothing in return. I had a feeling this may be the only church casserole—and everything it stands for—we would ever receive as a family, and eleven years later, it's true. Religion has fallen short for me in so many essential areas I explore in this book—morality, meaning, purpose, mortality, and awe—but the one thing that's been hard to find without religion is the sense of belonging I felt as a child in the church and haven't experienced since adolescence, when I began to doubt.

This book began with a question I've asked myself often over the years: *Where are more people like me?* I've spent a good majority of my days feeling like I don't quite fit in. Before I had kids, this feeling wasn't so much a dilemma as an opportunity. I love meeting new people, seeing new places, hearing about new ideas, stories, and experiences. But we live in a culture that designates whether people, places, and activities are "kid friendly," the implication being that young families aren't necessarily welcomed wherever we go. As if feeling like I didn't quite fit in before wasn't bad enough, now I'm never sure whether my entire party of five fits in, unless we're in a gated playground or petting zoo.

It helps that Chris and I met and started our family in a Midwestern town that serves as a sort of refuge for misfits. It also helps that we've moved to an entire state that seems to serve as a refuge for misfits. But still, American life, especially after becoming a parent, feels very compartmentalized. Work friends stay at work, school friends stay at school, and, with the exception of several we've been lucky to have, neighbors stay inside. We attend kid activities for the kids, adult activities for the adults, and never the two shall meet. I thought maybe I could find the community I was looking for online, through social media, blogs, and forums. But these relationships only go so far; they fall short in the complexity, endurance, and commitment I need to feel rooted in something deeper.

I didn't realize how badly I ached for a different kind of connection until, for the writing of this book, our family visited the local Unitarian Universalist fellowship to check out the religious education program. One of our first times there, a teenage boy stood up in front of the microphone to share a poem he'd written about his love for science. When he introduced himself as an atheist, my husband audibly sucked in his breath. I asked him about it after the service.

"I just felt instinctively afraid for him," Chris explained. "I can't imagine being able to say *I don't believe in God* in front of a big group like that, especially as a kid."

But we soon realized this is precisely what the group was about: people coming together regardless of age, color, orientation, background, lifestyle, or beliefs, who simply know that, as the UU website states, "Life is richer in community than when we go it alone."[1]

On our first visit, we were late, which is not unusual for us. We slipped in quietly, taking seats at the back of the room, while people I'd never seen before looked at us warmly, with smiling eyes. *You can fit in here.* As I took in the collective mood of the room, I was overwhelmed with tears. My children looked up at me the same way I used to look at my own mother when she cried at church.

"Why are you crying?" they whispered, like I did when I was a child.

"I can't explain it," I whispered back, like my mother did.

Why was I crying? I was nostalgic, to be sure. I was flooded with visceral memories: the way it feels to slip in late to a congregation; the way dark hymnals look on empty seats; the sound of silence in a room full of people who put the brakes on their day-to-day lives and sit together to consider things like integrity, hope, purpose, justice, and love. But it was also just the way I felt taking in a band of misfits. It's always in a group of people who are wildly different from one another that I feel like I belong. The young, the old, the dark, the light, the woman in kitten heels and a cardigan, the dude with tats in a tie-dye shirt. It wasn't *kid friendly*; it was *people friendly*. There was no certain kind or type—just genuine and accepting, like congregations I remember from my childhood, only no one was asking me to pledge or promise or confirm a thing.

My good friend Katie, who is married to a Nazarene pastor, once asked me what people do on Sundays when they don't go to church. She was being sincere, but I was annoyed. I got defensive. *Better things with our time,* I thought, but didn't say this out loud, and I gave her a list of noble-sounding, upstanding activities: family brunches, bike rides, hikes, museum visits, rescue missions to find ducks caught in oil spills and wash them with dish soap. *We do so many things.*

But I realize now that I misunderstood her question. Katie wasn't asking me to literally recount our Sunday mornings and what we do with our time. She was wondering what kind of substitute people find when they don't have a practice in place to connect with others over deep matters of existence. Those are the kinds of connections that sustain us as we make our way through life, getting cut off in traffic, standing in line at the grocery store, reading the latest heart-wrenching headline, wondering, *If this is humanity, how in the world do I fit in?*

As I looked into sources and ideas outside of religion to help shape ways I can explore timeless questions with my children, I began to pick up on a pattern that can be summarized in two words: other people. As in, how do I learn about morality? *Other people.* What is the number-one trigger of awe? *Other people.* Who can I turn to in times of grief and suffering? *Other people.* What gives life meaning? *Other people.* Why is tradition important? *Other people.*

But in order to learn as much from *other people* as possible, our exposure needs to be diverse. While I value our friendships with other families and parents, sometimes it feels like we're on an island. And considering it's our fast-growing kids that bind us together, I fear the island is sinking. Outside of churches, not many organizations bring together the beautiful, rich mixture of people from all walks of life. Add into this mix an intentional practice of thinking and doing bigger than ourselves, and maybe this explains my tears when I visited the UU fellowship.

The thing is, it takes some intention and persistence to find the kind of community we miss by being outside of religion, and the first step is just to know what we're missing in the first place. While my family hasn't committed regularly to the UU fellowship, our sporadic visits do bring attention to certain needs: for me, it's the kind of deep, sincere connection with other people that brings tears to my eyes; for Chris, it's a reminder that when we don't commit to a contemplative practice with a structure in place, it much too easily slips by the wayside.

This book began as many do: I decided to write a book I wanted to read. I knew from the headlines, statistics, and anecdotes that more Americans are leaving religion than any other time in our history, but I couldn't find much on how having kids can add turbulence to the flight. In an age when we're used to expressing and absorbing complicated issues in the space of a handheld screen, I knew this journey needed more time and attention.

It started when my kids asked questions and I realized I had so much to learn. Their questions urged me to break open our bubble of family life, visit some inspiring places, and meet some incredible people. In this time, I've learned that I'm not so alone after all; groups like the American Humanist Association, American Ethical Union, and Foundation Beyond Belief are increasing in numbers, providing the type of reflective structure, community, and opportunity for service we've been missing while being a positive force for change. During the writing of this book, we've discovered Camp Quest, a sleepaway camp dedicated to freethought that began in 1996 with a small group in Boone County, Kentucky, which has since grown across North America, the United Kingdom, Switzerland, and Norway. Our older two attended the camp located in Northern California and came home with rave reviews, already planning for next year.

We are a community rising and creating a future for our children. Encourage their thirst for knowledge. Find answers together. Inspire them to keep seeking, and let them know they're not alone.

NOTES

INTRODUCTION

1. Oxford English Dictionary, https://en.oxforddictionaries.com/definition/spirit.

2. Michael Lipka, "A Closer Look at America's Rapidly Growing Religious 'Nones,'" Pew Research Center, May 13, 2015, http://www.pewresearch.org/fact-tank/2015/05/13/a-closer-look-at-americas-rapidly-growing-religious-nones/.

3. https://en.oxforddictionaries.com/definition/apostate.

CHAPTER 1

1. Daniel J. Siegel and Mary Hartzell, *Parenting from the Inside Out: How a Deeper Self-Understanding Can Help You Raise Children Who Thrive* (New York: J. P. Tarcher/Putnam, 2003).

2. Dale McGowan, *Parenting beyond Belief: On Raising Ethical, Caring Kids without Religion* (New York: American Management Association, 2007).

3. Michael Krasny, *Spiritual Envy: An Agnostic's Quest* (Novato, CA: New World Library, 2010).

4. Kahlil Gibran, *The Prophet* (New York: Knopf, 1952).

CHAPTER 2

1. Phil Zuckerman, *Living the Secular Life: New Answers to Old Questions* (New York: Penguin Press, 2014).

CHAPTER 3

1. "Worldwide, Many See Belief in God Essential to Morality," Pew Research Center, March 13, 2014, http://www.pewglobal.org/2014/03/13/worldwide-many -see-belief-in-god-as-essential-to-morality.

2. James 2:10, KJV.

3. Phil Zuckerman, "How Secular Family Values Stack Up," *Los Angeles Times*, January 14, 2015, http://www.latimes.com/nation/la-oe-0115-zuckerman -secular-parenting-20150115-story.html.

4. Greg M. Epstein, *Good without God: What a Billion Nonreligious People Do Believe* (New York: Willian Morrow, 2009).

5. Karen Armstrong, *The Great Transformation: The Beginning of Our Religious Traditions* (New York: Knopf, 2006).

6. Claire Lerner and Rebecca Parlakian, "How to Help Your Child Develop Empathy," Zero to Three, February 1, 2016, https://www.zerotothree.org/ resources/5-how-to-help-your-child-develop-empathy.

7. Epstein, *Good without God.*

8. Ibid.

9. Jon J. Muth and Leo Tolstoy, *The Three Questions* (New York: Scholastic Press, 2002).

10. Dalai Lama, *Ethics for the New Millennium* (New York: Riverhead Press, 1999).

11. Ibid.

12. Shauna L. Shapiro and Chris White, *Mindful Discipline: A Loving Approach to Setting Limits and Raising an Emotionally Intelligent Child* (Oakland, CA: New Harbinger, 2014).

13. Pema Chödrön, *Start Where You Are: A Guide to Compassionate Living* (Boston: Shambhala, 1994).

CHAPTER 4

1. Sara Weissman, "Is It Pretty Outside? Then You're Less Likely to Go to Church," *Washington Post*, August 6, 2015, https://www.washingtonpost .com/national/religion/is-it-pretty-outside-then-youre-less-likely-to-go-to -church/2015/08/06/3ff677a2-3c73-11e5-a312-1a6452ac77d2_story.html.

2. Phil Zuckerman, *Living the Secular Life: New Answers to Old Questions* (New York: Penguin Press, 2014).

3. Dacher Keltner and Jonathan Haidt, "Approaching Awe, a Moral, Spiritual, and Aesthetic Emotion," *Cognition & Emotion* 17, no. 2 (2003): 297–314. doi: 10.1080/02699930302297.

4. Paul K. Piff, Pia Dietze, Matthew Feinberg, Daniel M. Stancato, and Dacher Keltner, "Awe, the Small Self, and Prosocial Behavior," *Journal of Personality and Social Psychology* 108, no. 6 (2015): 883–99.

5. Ibid.

6. Andy Tix, "Nurturing Awe in Kids," *Psychology Today*, September 21, 2015, https://www.psychologytoday.com/blog/the-pursuit-peace/201509/nurturing -awe-in-kids.

7. Keltner and Haidt, "Approaching Awe."

8. Annaka Harris, *I Wonder* (Four Elephants Press, 2013).

9. Ibid.

10. Ibid.

CHAPTER 5

1. https://www.childrensgriefawarenessday.org/cgad2/pdf/griefstatistics.pdf.

2. Wolf Erlbruch and Catherine Chidgey, *Duck, Death, and the Tulip* (Minneapolis: Gecko Press, distributed in the United States by Lerner Publishing Group, 2011).

3. Joanna Macy and Anita Barrows, *A Year with Rilke: Daily Readings from the Best of Rainer Maria Rilke* (New York: HarperOne, 2009).

4. Elisabeth Kübler-Ross, *On Death and Dying* (New York: Macmillan, 1969).

5. Wendy T. Russell, *Relax, It's Just God: How and Why to Talk to Your Kids about Religion When You're Not Religious* (Los Angeles: Brown Paper Press, 2015).

CHAPTER 6

1. Jon J. Muth, *Zen Shorts* (New York: Scholastic Press, 2005).

2. Annie Dillard, *The Writing Life* (New York: Harper & Row, 1989).

3. Adam Kaplin and Laura Anzaldi, "New Movement in Neuroscience: A Purpose-Driven Life," *Cerebrum*, May 2015, https://www.ncbi.nlm.nih.gov/pmc/ articles/PMC4564234/; Patricia A. Boyle, Lisa L. Barnes, Aron S. Buchman, and David A. Bennett, "Purpose in Life Is Associated with Mortality among Commu-

nity-Dwelling Older Persons," *Psychosomatic Medicine* 71, no. 5 (2009): 574–79. doi:10.1097/psy.0b013e3181a5a7c0.

4. Carey Wallace, "How to Help Your Kids Find a Purpose," *Time*, November 10, 2015, http://time.com/4105664/how-to-help-your-kids-find-a-purpose/.

5. Viktor E. Frankl, *Man's Search for Meaning* (Boston: Beacon Press, 2006).

6. Ibid.

7. Ibid.

8. M. F. Steger, P. Frazier, S. Oishi, and M. Kaler, "The Meaning in Life Questionnaire: Assessing the Presence of and Search for Meaning in Life," *Journal of Counseling Psychology* 53, no. 1 (2006): 80–93. doi:10.1037/0022-0167.53.1.80.

9. S. Katherine Nelson, Kostadin Kushlev, and Sonja Lyubomirsky, "The Pains and Pleasures of Parenting: When, Why, and How Is Parenthood Associated with More or Less Well-Being?" *Psychological Bulletin* 140, no. 3 (2014): 846–95. doi:10.1037/a0035444.

10. Roy F. Baumeister, Kathleen D. Vohs, Jennifer L. Aaker, and Emily N. Garbinsky, "Some Key Differences between a Happy Life and a Meaningful Life," *Journal of Positive Psychology* 8, no. 6 (2013): 505–16. doi:10.1080/17439760.2 013.830764.

11. Frankl, *Man's Search for Meaning*.

12. Frank Martela and Michael F. Steger, "The Three Meanings of Meaning in Life: Distinguishing Coherence, Purpose, and Significance," *Journal of Positive Psychology* 11, no. 5 (2016): 531–45. doi:10.1080/17439760.2015.1137623.

13. Frankl, *Man's Search for Meaning*.

14. Ibid.

15. Jay N. Giedd, "The Teen Brain: Insights from Neuroimaging," *Journal of Adolescent Health* 42, no. 4 (2008): 335–43. doi:10.1016/j.jadohealth.2008.01.007.

16. Rick Weissbourd et al., "The Children We Mean to Raise: The Real Messages Adults Are Sending about Values," *Making Caring Common Project*, 2014. http://mcc.gse.harvard.edu/the-children-we-mean-to-raise.

17. Ibid.

18. Frankl, *Man's Search for Meaning*.

CHAPTER 7

1. http://www.census.gov/newsroom/press-releases/2015/cb15-47.html.

2. J. M. Burkart, S. B. Hrdy, and C. P. Van Schaik, "Cooperative Breeding and Human Cognitive Evolution," *Evolutionary Anthropology: Issues, News, and Reviews* 18, no. 5 (2009): 175–86. doi:10.1002/evan.20222.

3. Marshall P. Duke, Amber Lazarus, and Robyn Fivush, "Knowledge of Family History as a Clinically Useful Index of Psychological Well-Being and Prognosis: A Brief Report," *Psychotherapy: Theory, Research, Practice, Training* 45, no. 2 (2008): 268–72. doi:10.1037/0033-3204.45.2.268.

4. Bruce S. Feiler, "The Stories That Bind Us," *New York Times*, March 15, 2013.

CHAPTER 8

1. Maria Popova, "The Difference between Routine and Ritual," *Brain Pickings*, https://www.brainpickings.org/2015/02/13/routine-ritual-anne-lamott-stitches/.

2. Krista Tippett, "A School of Life for Atheists," *On Being*, audio podcast, September 21, 2016, http://www.onbeing.org/program/alain-de-botton-school -life-atheists/4821.

3. Dale McGowan, *Parenting beyond Belief: On Raising Ethical, Caring Kids without Religion* (New York: American Management Association, 2007).

4. Arnold van Gennep, *The Rites of Passage* (Chicago: University of Chicago Press, 1960).

CONCLUSION

1. http://www.uua.org/beliefs/what-we-believe/higher-power.

BIBLIOGRAPHY

Armstrong, Karen. *The Great Transformation: The Beginning of Our Religious Traditions*. New York: Knopf, 2006.

Baumeister, Roy F., Kathleen D. Vohs, Jennifer L. Aaker, and Emily N. Garbinsky. "Some Key Differences between a Happy Life and a Meaningful Life." *Journal of Positive Psychology* 8, no. 6 (2013): 505–16. doi:10.1080/17439760.2013.8 30764.

Boyle, Patricia A., Lisa L. Barnes, Aron S. Buchman, and David A. Bennett. "Purpose in Life Is Associated with Mortality among Community-Dwelling Older Persons." *Psychosomatic Medicine* 71, no. 5 (2009): 574–79. doi:10.1097/psy.0b013e3181a5a7c0.

Burkart, J. M., S. B. Hrdy, and C. P. Van Schaik. "Cooperative Breeding and Human Cognitive Evolution." *Evolutionary Anthropology: Issues, News, and Reviews* 18, no. 5 (2009): 175–86. doi:10.1002/evan.20222.

Chödrön, Pema. *Start Where You Are: A Guide to Compassionate Living*. Boston: Shambhala, 1994.

Dillard, Annie. *The Writing Life*. New York: Harper & Row, 1989.

Duke, Marshall P., Amber Lazarus, and Robyn Fivush. "Knowledge of Family History as a Clinically Useful Index of Psychological Well-Being and Prognosis: A Brief Report." *Psychotherapy: Theory, Research, Practice, Training* 45, no. 2 (2008): 268–72. doi:10.1037/0033-3204.45.2.268.

Epstein, Greg M. *Good without God: What a Billion Nonreligious People Do Believe*. New York: William Morrow, 2009.

Erlbruch, Wolf, and Catherine Chidgey. *Duck, Death, and the Tulip*. Minneapolis: Gecko Press, distributed in the United States by Lerner Publishing Group, 2011.

Feiler, Bruce S. "The Stories That Bind Us." *New York Times*, March 15, 2013.

Frankl, Viktor E. *Man's Search for Meaning*. Boston: Beacon Press, 2006.

Gennep, Arnold van. *The Rites of Passage*. Chicago: University of Chicago Press, 1960.

Gibran, Kahlil. *The Prophet*. New York: Knopf, 1952.

Giedd, Jay N. "The Teen Brain: Insights from Neuroimaging." *Journal of Adolescent Health* 42, no. 4 (2008): 335–43. doi:10.1016/j.jadohealth.2008.01.007.

Harris, Annaka. *I Wonder*. Four Elephants Press, 2013.

Kaplin, Adam, and Laura Anzaldi. "New Movement in Neuroscience: A Purpose-Driven Life." *Cerebrum*, May 2015. https://www.ncbi.nlm.nih.gov/pmc/articles/PMC4564234/.

Keltner, Dacher, and Jonathan Haidt. "Approaching Awe, a Moral, Spiritual, and Aesthetic Emotion." *Cognition & Emotion* 17, no. 2 (2003): 297–314. doi:10.1080/02699930302297.

Krasny, Michael. *Spiritual Envy: An Agnostic's Quest*. Novato, CA: New World Library, 2010.

Kübler-Ross, Elisabeth. *On Death and Dying*. New York: Macmillan, 1969.

Lama, Dalai. *Ethics for the New Millennium*. New York: Riverhead Press, 1999.

Lerner, Claire, and Rebecca Parlakian. "How to Help Your Child Develop Empathy." Zero to Three, February 1, 2016. https://www.zerotothree.org/resources/5-how-to-help-your-child-develop-empathy.

Lipka, Michael. "A Closer Look at America's Rapidly Growing Religious 'Nones.'" Pew Research Center, May 13, 2015. http://www.pewresearch.org/fact-tank/2015/05/13/a-closer-look-at-americas-rapidly-growing-religious-nones/.

Macy, Joanna, and Anita Barrows. *A Year with Rilke: Daily Readings from the Best of Rainer Maria Rilke*. New York: HarperOne, 2009.

Martela, Frank, and Michael F. Steger. "The Three Meanings of Meaning in Life: Distinguishing Coherence, Purpose, and Significance." *Journal of Positive Psychology* 11, no. 5 (2016): 531–45. doi:10.1080/17439760.2015.1137623.

McGowan, Dale. *In Faith and In Doubt: How Religious Believers and Nonbelievers Can Create Strong Marriages and Loving Families*. New York: American Management Association, 2014.

McGowan, Dale. *Parenting beyond Belief: On Raising Ethical, Caring Kids without Religion*. New York: American Management Association, 2007.

McGowan, Dale. *Raising Freethinkers: A Practical Guide for Parenting beyond Belief*. New York: AMACOM, American Management Association, 2009.

Muth, Jon J. *Zen Shorts*. New York: Scholastic Press, 2005.

Muth, Jon J., and Leo Tolstoy. *The Three Questions*. New York: Scholastic Press, 2002.

Nelson, S. Katherine, Kostadin Kushlev, and Sonja Lyubomirsky. "The Pains and Pleasures of Parenting: When, Why, and How Is Parenthood Associated with More or Less Well-Being?" *Psychological Bulletin* 140, no. 3 (2014): 846–95. doi:10.1037/a0035444.

Piff, Paul K., Pia Dietze, Matthew Feinberg, Daniel M. Stancato, and Dacher Keltner. "Awe, the Small Self, and Prosocial Behavior." *Journal of Personality and Social Psychology* 108, no. 6 (2015): 883–99. doi:10.1037/pspi0000018.

Popova, Maria. "The Difference between Routine and Ritual." *Brain Pickings*. https://www.brainpickings.org/2015/02/13/routine-ritual-anne-lamott-stitches/.

Russell, Wendy T. *Relax, It's Just God: How and Why to Talk to Your Kids about Religion When You're Not Religious*. Los Angeles: Brown Paper Press, 2015.

Shapiro, Shauna L., and Chris White. *Mindful Discipline: A Loving Approach to Setting Limits and Raising an Emotionally Intelligent Child*. Oakland, CA: New Harbinger, 2014.

Siegel, Daniel J., and Mary Hartzell. *Parenting from the Inside Out: How a Deeper Self-Understanding Can Help You Raise Children Who Thrive*. New York: J. P. Tarcher/Putnam, 2003.

Steger, M. F., P. Frazier, S. Oishi, and M. Kaler. "The Meaning in Life Questionnaire: Assessing the Presence of and Search for Meaning in Life." *Journal of Counseling Psychology* 53, no. 1 (2006): 80–93. doi:10.1037/0022-0167.53.1.80.

Tippett, Krista. "A School of Life for Atheists." *On Being*. Audio Podcast, September 21, 2016. http://www.onbeing.org/program/alain-de-botton-school-life-atheists/4821.

Tix, Andy. "Nurturing Awe in Kids." *Psychology Today*, September 21, 2015. https://www.psychologytoday.com/blog/the-pursuit-peace/201509/nurturing-awe-in-kids.

Wallace, Carey. "How to Help Your Kids Find a Purpose." *Time*, November 10, 2015. http://time.com/4105664/how-to-help-your-kids-find-a-purpose/.

Weissbourd, Rick, and Stephanie Jones, with Trisha Ross Anderson, Jennifer Kahn, and Mark Russell. "The Children We Mean to Raise: The Real Messages Adults Are Sending about Values." *Making Caring Common Project*, 2014. http://mcc.gse.harvard.edu/the-children-we-mean-to-raise.

Weissman, Sara. "Is It Pretty Outside? Then You're Less Likely to Go to Church." *Washington Post*, August 6, 2015. https://www.washingtonpost.com/national/religion/is-it-pretty-outside-then-youre-less-likely-to-go-to-church/2015/08/06/3ff677a2-3c73-11e5-a312-1a6452ac77d2_story.html.

"Worldwide, Many See Belief in God Essential to Morality." Pew Research Center, March 13, 2014. http://www.pewglobal.org/2014/03/13/worldwide-many-see-belief-in-god-as-essential-to-morality.

Zuckerman, Phil. "How Secular Family Values Stack Up." *Los Angeles Times*, January 14, 2015. http://www.latimes.com/nation/la-oe-0115-zuckerman-secular-parenting-20150115-story.html.

Zuckerman, Phil. *Living the Secular Life: New Answers to Old Questions*. New York: Penguin Press, 2014.

INDEX

ABOUT THE AUTHOR

Maria Polonchek is a Kansas native living in the San Francisco Bay Area. She has published award-winning poetry, short stories, and essays and began writing extensively on the motherhood experience after having twins in 2005. She now has three children and has written for the literary magazine *Brain, Child*; contributed to the anthology *Have Milk, Will Travel*; and chronicled her experience parenting outside religion for *The Greater Good Science Center*, *The Friendly Atheist*, and *Brain, Mother*. In addition to thinking, reading, and writing about parenting, she is passionate about wellness, mindfulness, the outdoors, music, art, and the way all of these things relate to issues of social justice.